TOO SMALL FOR PHYSIOTHERAPY

TOO SMALL FOR PHYSIOTHERAPY

Professor Grace Dorey MBE

The Book Guild Ltd

First published in Great Britain in 2021 by
The Book Guild Ltd
9 Priory Business Park
Wistow Road, Kibworth
Leicestershire, LE8 0RX
Freephone: 0800 999 2982
www.bookguild.co.uk
Email: info@bookguild.co.uk
Twitter: @bookguild

Copyright © 2021 Professor Grace Dorey MBE

The right of Professor Grace Dorey MBE to be identified as the author of this
work has been asserted by her in accordance with the
Copyright, Design and Patents Act 1988.

All rights reserved. No part of this publication may be
reproduced, transmitted, or stored in a retrieval system, in any form or by any means,
without permission in writing from the publisher, nor be otherwise circulated in
any form of binding or cover other than that in which it is published and without
a similar condition being imposed on the subsequent purchaser.

Typeset in 11pt Minion Pro

Printed and bound by CPI Group (UK) Ltd, Croydon, CR0 4YY

ISBN 978 1913913 281

British Library Cataloguing in Publication Data.
A catalogue record for this book is available from the British Library.

For my daughter, Claire, my son, Martin,
and my granddaughters, Maggie and Charlie.
And, of course, to Nick.

'A truly delightful account of Professor Dorey's fascinating young life, which reveals the strong influence her family had on her life. Her self-deprecating manner is amusing and modest. I became so involved in her story and could identify closely with many of her experiences.'

Jenny Buchan, English Teacher.

The Blundell Family Tree

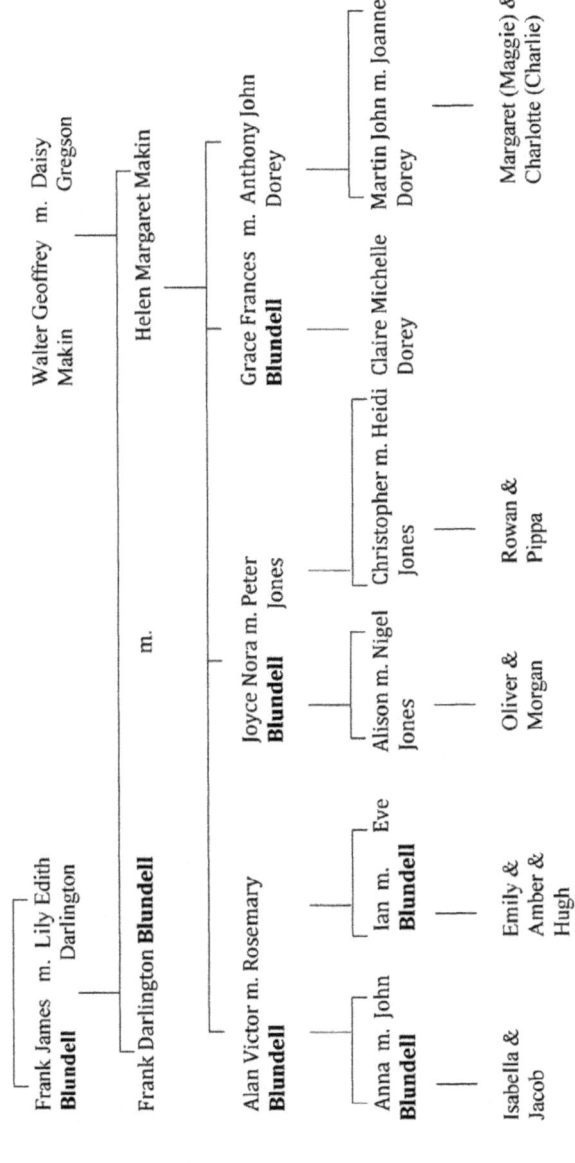

Why I Have Written This Book

I was brought up by parents who were both dedicated teachers, who hoped that I would follow their example and teach too. Despite their knowledge of other career pathways, I was not encouraged to consider any other avenue. If I had been allowed to pursue my dream, I would have followed my first love and been a ballerina. It was not to be.

Somehow, I was destined to be a physiotherapist in a career stretching fifty-four years, which I thoroughly enjoyed. Each patient brought a different challenge and it was a privilege to be able to use my skills to help to alleviate their pain and disability. I have written about my time as a physiotherapist in a book designed to make the reader smile titled *Rubbed Up the Wrong Way: A Physiotherapist's Story*, so this book is a prequel and candidly relates to my young and innocent life before I became a physiotherapist.

I have written this reflective manuscript while adhering to the Irish governmental lockdown directions in an effort to stay safe and prevent a further spread of the ghastly coronavirus, Covid-19. I have had many hours of pleasure revisiting my past and I hope that it will interest you as much as it has amused me.

Grace Dorey

Chapter 1

War Baby

There was a break in the bombing on 6th October, when my father drove his Standard 10 flat-out to Fairlight Nursing Home in Whetstone, so that Mother could give birth to me, her third child in three years and most definitely her last. When my mother introduced me to anyone, she always called me 'her baby', while I suffered this indignity with increasingly resigned stoicism well into and beyond my adolescent years! The year was 1940, so the Second World War was raging furiously, although my mother said that the German Luftwaffe bombers, so menacing in the battle of Britain, were absent the day that I entered the world, but even so I became known from then on as a 'war baby'. It is inconceivable to think that I, a staunch pacifist, could possibly hold the 'war' moniker. My parents christened me Grace (my mother said that she would tell me one day why I was called Grace – but she never did), a name with which I am not unhappy but one that reminded me of a generation of great-aunts and the singer Gracie Fields, though I liked the idea of being associated with the beautiful Grace Kelly! Would you believe it, now, I happily sign myself Great Aunt Grace to my great nieces and great nephews, as it has a certain ring to it.

My mother, Helen Margaret Makin, ditched her first name when she was young as she disliked the sound of it and from then on was always known as Margaret. She had left motherhood rather late, as she was thirty-six when I was born, whilst my father was an impressive forty years of age. They met when they were walking in opposite directions to the different schools where they were both teaching; gradually a flutter became a smile which developed into a chat which led to them 'walking out' together. My mother was on the small side and had glorious curly brown hair framing beautiful blue eyes flashing behind tinted frameless glasses worn to correct short-sightedness and a mild squint. My father, Frank Darlington Blundell, was average height, slim as a beanpole (he was lucky as his weight stayed the same for the whole of his long life) with dark brown hair and the Blundell blue eyes which faded with age. When they were married my mother had to retain her maiden name and wore her wedding ring round her neck, as married women were not allowed to hold teaching posts in those days. How different from now, when the majority of female teachers are married.

We lived in a large semi-detached brick-built house (circa 1937) in Totteridge, North London, with three bedrooms, one with a bay window at the front of the house for my parents, who shared a double bed until my father contracted cystitis, when they had single beds for the rest of their marriage. How sad is that? I learned the reason why I was the last child when I was putting my mother's clean laundry in her underwear drawer and found a thick pink rubber condom wrapped carefully in talcum powder. It was as thick as a bicycle tyre, for goodness' sake; my father would not have been able to feel a thing. How different from today's super-lite latex products promising strength, thinness and heightened sensation. Indeed, now you can even buy vegan condoms if you don't want animal products up you!

On with the story; there was one bedroom in the front of the house for my brother, Alan, and one overlooking the garden that I shared with my sister, Joyce. Downstairs we had a front room with a bay window, used only for best occasions, with a brownish uncut moquette three-piece suite and a coal fire, where on special days we toasted crumpets following a ferociously fought fight for the longest toasting fork to prevent our fingers from being singed. At the back of the house there was a dining room with a mahogany dining table with permanently extended flaps, six mahogany dining chairs with (you've guessed it) brown moquette seats, two very uncomfortable easy chairs with wooden arms, which were wedding presents from staff at my parents' schools, and joyous French windows opening out to our garden. The kitchen had a dresser with a drop-down enamel shelf for making pastry, a small coke boiler, which heated the water, a primitive gas cooker on legs, an Ascot water heater over a wooden draining board, a large rather chipped butler's sink and a pine table (with flaps) which was scrubbed to one inch of its life to supposedly sterilise it. There was no working surface for the preparation of food other than this table, to which was fixed the runner beans cutter, the mincer and the mangle, but not all at the same time!

If my father had served abroad in the war, I would not have been conceived, but as he was a valued teacher, he was active in the Home Guard and obviously active at home too! In later years, Pop said that the Home Guard was *exactly* like the TV programme *Dad's Army*, where they saw no Germans, marauding or otherwise, but played what they considered a vital role in the defence of the country, largely by spending most of their time holed up in the local pub. I never saw his rifle, but when I was older I found his helmet and gas mask in the cupboard under the stairs. Apparently, I was too young to have a gas mask so would have perished in a gas attack! As my father was teetotal, he was detailed to sit outside The Orange Tree hostelry in Totteridge to alert his mates, not if a German snuck up, but if a member of the ARP (Air Raid Precautions) dared to come within smelling distance. One night, he was left alone for hours freezing to death in a church graveyard, clad only in his inadequate khaki uniform, when his inebriated mates forgot all about him and, rather absentmindedly and very merrily, rolled home.

On days when Pop was not playing soldiers, he volunteered to help in the soup kitchens in the East End of London, providing sustenance for those families whose homes had been bombed and who were sadly made homeless. Many of the survivors had not only lost family and friends but sustained gruesome injuries in the dreadful devastation of the capital city.

Everywhere at night was pitch black outside unless there was a full moon, as street lights were turned off and everyone's windows were covered with cheap blackout curtains; it was the role of the ARP to let residents know if there was so much as a chink of light shining outwards, which would be visible from the air and alert German pilots as to the vicinity of a residential area. The ARP were resplendent in their uniforms consisting of dark blue overalls with distinctive domed steel helmets, which were a jolly shade of black sporting a large white painted 'W' on the front. Each member had access to a gas mask, a three-metre-long pike to test unsafe ceilings, a wooden gas rattle similar to a football rattle to warn of a gas attack, a handbell to ring the all-clear, a stirrup pump, hose and bucket to extinguish the weeniest of fires, and a first aid kit containing a triangular bandage with, I guess, an extensive range of possible medical uses.

My Auntie Freda told me that when the sirens gave a warning of an air raid, Alan and Joyce were taken hurriedly through a gate in the fence to the safety of the concrete air-raid shelter next door, while I was left in a carrycot underneath the kitchen table, which presumably was considered sturdy enough to protect me should the house fall down! Luckily, it didn't, and we got off lightly, as the only damage sustained was in a field at the end of the road, when a doodlebug exploded nearby, leaving a deep angry crater which shattered our front bay windows so that upstairs, broken glass covered my mother's dressing table and downstairs it smothered the sofa. To make matters worse, the explosion also caused an avalanche of soot to fall down from the chimney and spread all over the carpet in the sacred lounge. Another doodlebug exploded in Longland Drive, which again was rather too close for comfort. After these explosions, Mother found that the glaze was cracked on all the pieces of our best dinner service. A small price to pay considering the appalling devastation and extensive loss of life in other areas of the country.

When I was young and taken up to London, there were large wooden screens around all the bomb sites. I was told off by Mother for peeping between the hoardings to look at the bomb damage, which had left vast craters that tragically replaced people's homes and offices. It was many, many years before the property in London was rebuilt.

My earliest recollection was being left in a pram in the wooden summer house at the bottom of our long garden in leafy Totteridge and seeing the finger of a neighbour wiggle up and down through a knothole in the fence to try and stop me crying. I guess I was abandoned so that my mother was unable to hear my hearty wails from the house, though looking back it seemed to me it was without any consideration for the peace and serenity of the finger-wiggler.

I also remember that when I was a toddler, I had to wear a horrid brown leather belt with a nasty knob to press my tummy button back in. It was kept in the laundry basket, for goodness' sake! When I purposely 'forgot' to wear it, there was always a family member more than willing to remind me. It was an evil contraption which I hated and it is a wonder that I haven't been afflicted with some lingering psychological neurosis. Perhaps I have? I still have to hold my stomach when I cough or sneeze and to my horror, my umbilicus turned inside out when I was pregnant. Today, umbilical hernias can be treated with minor surgery but this was not considered back then.

We had a 'family doctor' called Dr Hicks, who was 'on call' permanently seven days a week for his own patients and always did home visits when we were ill. One time, he was called in to see me when I was in a cot in my parents' bedroom as I had a worrying rash. Before he left, he squeezed my nose playfully, smiled and said goodbye, so as he was walking out of the room, I beckoned to him to come back then squeezed his nose so hard that he *yelped* in pain. I wondered if he ever tweaked a child's nose again! Certainly not mine. Family doctors became family friends and Pop used to give him a framed sketch that he had done as a present to thank him for seeing us. I wonder if this was in lieu of payment in the days before free healthcare, as it was not until 1948 that the NHS was founded by Aneurin Bevan, the Minister of Health in Attlee's post-war Labour government. Nowadays, there is free healthcare, which is brilliant, but the days of having a 'family doctor' have gone, as most general practitioners belong to a group practice and patients may see another doctor if their registered doctor is unavailable. Also, there are precious few home visits now, so patients who are seriously ill have to dial 999 and get an ambulance to take them to hospital.

The three of us suffered from all the usual childhood illnesses, such as mumps, measles, German measles, whooping cough and chickenpox. If one of us became ill, it was inevitable that the others would follow suit a few days later. It must have been so difficult for Mother; no wonder she suffered from so many headaches. Chickenpox was the worst illness of all because we were told not to scratch the awful incessant itching or we would get scars, so we were liberally anointed with calamine lotion to stop the discomfort and happily we remained scar-free. Nowadays, most of these childhood illnesses are stamped out in the UK as, fortunately, children have MMR vaccinations for mumps, measles and rubella (German measles); in 1960 an orally administered polio vaccine was developed and administered on a sugar lump to rid the UK population of polio; and in 2014 flu vaccination started to become available. Fortunately, there are vaccinations against Covid-19, which has caused this ghastly pandemic with so much suffering and extensive loss of life around the world.

Our home remedies were kept in an *unlocked* bathroom cabinet and, I guess, many containers are now collector's pieces. Mother took aspirin-phenacetin-caffeine (APC), a compound analgesic for her frequent headaches until phenacetin was banned in the 1960s, because it caused renal disease. Occasionally, she took 'Regoids' laxative tablets to keep her bowels regular and 'Milk of Magnesia' or 'Eno's for indigestion. She was very excited when penicillin came onto the market in 1942, as it was superior to the antibacterial sulphonamide 'M & B' that was popular then. Pop found the antiseptic ointment 'Zam-Buck' and antiseptic liquid 'TCP' to be effective for skin wounds, and we were intrigued that he gargled 'TCP' when he had a sore throat. If we had a sore throat we were given the lovely 'Allenbury's Glycerine and Blackcurrant Pastilles', now marketed under the name Grether and sadly made sugar-free. Pop was not popular when he used some sort of embrocation for his sore muscles and joints, as it stank beyond belief rather like horse liniment. We had 'Golden Eye' ointment for sore eyes, but it was withdrawn due to its mercury content and re-introduced in 1992 with a different antiseptic. As children, we quite liked having 'Vicks VapoRub' applied to our chests if we had a chesty cold, and we used the *same* 'Vicks Nasal Inhaler' to stick up our noses and clear our sinuses. Can you believe it! One inhaler shared by the whole family possibly spread the infection further! At least we didn't have goose fat rubbed onto our chests and covered with a vest (or brown paper) at the beginning of the winter like our grannies endured to prevent chesty colds.

It seems as if I, being an (expendable) third child, was left to my own devices as my mother told me that when I was three years old, she was appalled to see me sitting happily on the roof of the six-foot-high summer house. Apparently, I had climbed up the open-work trellis 'windows' until I reached my goal. When I was brought down, apparently, I said: 'It was a bit hilly!'

When I was going on four years of age, I, the intrepid climber, was needed to shin up a long, wobbly wooden ladder and slip through an upper skylight window to enter the house of the finger-wiggler, who had inadvertently locked herself out. There was no helmet or safety net for me, just someone to prevent the rather unsteady ladder from slipping and a collection of concerned commentators giving me considerable encouragement. I can still remember feeling very important when I performed this feat and proudly opened her front door. Recently, Emily, my great niece aged sixteen years, shinned up a ladder to enter an open top lavatory window when the family were locked out, but unfortunately, she became stuck, like Winnie the Pooh, being quite unable to go either in or out! She could still be there now, if a kindly neighbour hadn't climbed the ladder behind her and nobly pushed her into the loo.

In 1945, when I was four and a half, VE Day (Victory in Europe Day) in the United Kingdom was celebrated in Laurel Way, Totteridge, with flags, bunting and much festivity in a street party, even though food was still rationed and extremely limited. Pop unfurled a dusty Union Jack flag from the upper recesses of the garage and fixed it proudly onto the front of the house. The street party was celebrated by all the neighbours, even though many of the military had died or failed to return home while serving their country. The servicemen who were serving or imprisoned in Japan were still in the Far East and arrived back in Britain after Japan surrendered on August 15th, 1945 so this date is remembered each year as VJ Day (Victory over Japan Day).

I remember the white dresses with a fine red and blue check that Mother had made for both Joyce and me to celebrate this momentous occasion. In the evening, when I was sent to bed, the adults danced in the road to music blaring out from celluloid records on a neighbour's gramophone. The energetic lindy hop, a jazz dance which had arrived from America, was all the rage.

On 8th May 2020, it was seventy-five years since VE Day in the United Kingdom, so this anniversary was remembered up and down the country, even though the lockdown ordered by the government for protection from the super-virus Covid-19 prevented the joyful street parties like those held for the previously significant fifty-year anniversary. In 2020, despite being isolated and instructed to keep a distance of two metres from other people, many families made flags and bunting, picnicked in their front gardens, and joined together to sing war-time songs made popular by the late Dame Vera Lynn, the forces' sweetheart, such as 'We'll Meet Again' and '(There'll Be Bluebirds Over) The White Cliffs of Dover' in a demonstration of neighbourly comradeship. In this way, my granddaughters, Maggie and Charlie, enjoyed a brilliant interlude from being cocooned in Bude. Looking into the future, my children, Claire and Martin, and my grandchildren will see the VE Day centenary in twenty-five years' time. What a brilliant celebration that will be without the restrictions of lockdown imposed on everybody to fight the raging pandemic. I guess by then everyone will have an annual coronavirus vaccination in order to stay safe.

Just before the VE Day street party in 1945, I was invited to a celebration of a different kind. A friend of mine, whose name I am ashamed that I cannot remember, held her fourth birthday party in her home in Ventnor Drive. At the party tea, I was served orange squash in a delicate glass. You are probably ahead of me! With my baby teeth, I bit through the glass and was so horrified that I dashed out of the house and rushed home in tears. I expected trouble. For once, it was deemed not to be my fault, as my mother told me that it was silly to serve a drink in a glass to four-year-olds.

I recovered from this incident by playing in the garden, a garden which was 'shed city'. My father built a sturdy shed in each corner – well, one was a wooden greenhouse, which could be locked with a key. Alan used to take great delight in locking me in when I went in to pick a strawberry, so I screamed louder and louder and became hotter and hotter, even though I knew that no-one could hear me from the house, until he finally freed me. Then, a purpose-built chicken house was constructed along one side of the garden and later, on the opposite side, a rabbit hutch was fashioned for Joyce's pet rabbits, though either it was a tad faulty or the rabbits were wildly intelligent, as they were forever escaping, mostly at mealtimes, when we children would rush excitedly into the garden in an attempt to catch the escapees before they ate any rhubarb leaves, much to Mother's discomfort that we were leaving the table. The poor escaped creatures must have been scared senseless seeing three excited children bearing down on their disappearing cotton tails, but I remember these incidents as happy times that I spent with my siblings. Chasing rabbits was infinitely more exciting than sitting up sedately at the table having dinner with the family.

The rest of the garden, which was not occupied by sheds, was laid out to fruit and vegetables, so we were self-sufficient during the war and in the austere post-war years and enjoyed freshly picked seasonal produce. Now, I cannot eat a greengage without being drawn back to our garden in Totteridge, where these trees produced prolific fruit and we happily climbed ladders to harvest them. My father loved rhubarb, which he forced in upended bottomless metal buckets, so that we could enjoy the young pink shoots early in the season. In the greenhouse he grew tomatoes and strawberries, so it was always a delight to enter the greenhouse and pick either of them straight off the plant, first making sure that the key was on the inside of the door! There was a selection of gnarled Bramley apple trees and a profusion of redcurrant, blackcurrant and raspberry bushes. Also, he grew potatoes, runner beans, carrots, cabbages, peas, leeks and even the dreaded Brussel sprouts.

As if this was not enough, my father had an allotment over the road in a vacant house plot to provide even more produce for our post-wartime sustenance. Alan, Joyce and I were willing helpers on the allotment, though I don't know how much we contributed to actually growing the vegetables, but we did don Wellington boots and feel very important carrying an array of garden implements across the road for Father to use on his plot. We probably helped him to weed, as he gave us an old penny for a bucket full of weeds, even though we complained that we were being exploited and underpaid. When we were home, we used to sit in deck chairs on the lawn and 'top and tail' gooseberries using scissors, or shell peas and broad beans, all the while competing against one another or teasing each other if anyone was slacking.

The chicken eggs were either eaten or pickled in isinglass in a bucket in the shed and it was the children's job to put a hand into the cold, slimy water to retrieve them ready for cake-making. We tried everything to avoid this task – it still makes me shiver and go all goosy to think of it!

Chapter 2

The Three of Us

My mother found her energetic young family to be more than a handful and totally relied on my father to help bring us up. My mother was the disciplinarian of the family, the controller, whereas my father was just the opposite being totally laid-back, preferring to be 'very useful' in the garage if things became heated. As he was descended from a long line of carpenters, he fashioned toys for us out of wood, painted in green for Alan, blue for Joyce and red for me. He had a love affair with wood and absolutely abhorred plastic. We proudly possessed wooden bats, jumping frames and stilts in our own primary colours. Later, we had similarly coloured scooters with rackety wooden wheels, which we were not allowed to play with outside on the pavement on a Sunday afternoon, when Mother took a much-needed nap. We were schooled to scoot first with one foot and then the other, in order to wear the soles of our leather shoes out evenly, as my father had taken on the role of the family cobbler and mended our footwear on a shoe-last in the garage. Cleverly, he fashioned new leather soles and added Blakey heel and toe tips for extra strength.

Our identifying colours were also important to distinguish our toothbrushes and our Gibbs toothpaste from each other. The solid dentifrice came concentrated in a hard, pink cake in a round green, blue or red tin, and it was designed to last twice as long as toothpaste and was a bargain at a cost of seven and a half old pence! We had to wet the hard cake with water and make our own paste. As you can imagine, there was a good deal of screaming and spitting on each other's toothbrushes when the three of us were cleaning our teeth at the same time.

When I was three, Joyce was four and Alan was knocking on five years of age, Mother started a nursery school in our dining room. My friend, Kay, from across the road was enrolled and became the first child to pay for this privileged education. Pop made little chairs, and tables for the kindergarten and also an array of wooden building blocks and sticks of various shapes painted in an array of bright colours. Mother made multiple cards with letters on for word-building and a selection of other cards with numbers on for counting, so I learned my literary skills and mathematics from home tuition. If the siren went off during our nursery education, we would rush into the air-raid shelter next door and in the dank, musty atmosphere, Mother would read a story to us.

Joyce and I used to have a story read to us at night before we went to bed, but if Mother was busy or too exhausted, Pop would be sent in. He made up his stories as he went along, and we became thoroughly frustrated and rather troubled when they never ended and we were promised that they would be continued the next night. He told us all about the pink butterfly, a story that never ever finished, and I had a sneaky feeling that he could not think of an ending, suitable or otherwise. It was not conducive to sleep, just the opposite as the wretched pink butterfly failed to either die, fly away or live happily ever after.

When we were older Pop read us the *Just So Stories* by Rudyard Kipling, so we learned how the elephant got its trunk, how the zebra got its stripes, how the rhino got his skin, how the leopard got its spots, how the camel got his hump and even how the whale got its throat, though I would have to read them again to know now. I can only remember that a crocodile pulled and pulled and pulled the elephant's nose until it became a trunk – a vividly memorable story. They all started with the wonderful phrase 'O my best beloved', and we not only loved hearing them, but even more we enjoyed seeing Pop returning to his childhood, as he was in his element reading them to us.

Gradually the demand for nursery education meant that Mother took over the Union Church hut across the road and established an unrivalled nursery school there, with two other teachers and up to a hundred pupils. She used a jelly pad duplicator (gelatine hectograph) to send letters to parents in the days before photocopiers were born. She kept the fees to a minimum, so that everyone could afford to send their children to her kindergarten. There was one film star who wanted to know if the fee was per term or per week! Mother said that she could always tell from the under-fives who was clever enough to go on to university. She also dismissed dyslexia as an illness, as she felt that these disadvantaged children had not been taught their word-building skills correctly.

At home, there was a small lawn where the three of us played games such as 'piggy in the middle' and French cricket in the summer. I was mostly to be found upside-down as I performed somersaults, handstands, backflips and cartwheels to my heart's content. In fact, if we were taken to any open spaces, I would perform handstands, turning over and over. When we went to Kew Gardens, it was the beautiful manicured lawns rather than the horticulture that delighted me, so that I could happily turn a series of uninterrupted cartwheels into infinity.

Alan and I were reprimanded by Mother for jumping off from the roof of one of the six-foot-high sheds onto the lawn. It was a shame to have this activity curtailed, as we had perfected our jumps so that we missed the crazy-paving pathway and landed neatly, or not so, on the grass. Looking back, this was an amazing achievement for a fearless four-year-old and it is a wonder that I didn't break any bones, ruin any joints or at the very least have a greenstick fracture. I must have been very bouncy.

Alan was always treated differently from his sisters; he had a red pedal car which he drove proudly round the garden while Joyce and I were given doll's prams. Mother said that Joyce would be a much better mother than me, as her doll was tucked up neatly in her pram while my pram was just a receptacle for junk! Perhaps I should have been given a garbage truck. Boys were allowed to get grubby while girls, quite unfairly, had to stay clean. I learned this lesson when I followed Alan to the Dollis brook, where he was happily floating down the river with his pals on a homemade raft. I joined in the fun, unaware of the vehement scolding that was awaiting me when I arrived home from Mother. Life was unfair. I still believe that children of both sexes should have equal opportunities and not be assigned to activities which are historically associated with their gender.

One Sunday evening, when my parents were in the church hut diagonally across the road, Joyce and I were left playing with my friend, Kay, while Alan was in his room. We girls decided to bounce up and down on the sofa in the front room, the room that was only used for 'best'. This was enormous fun but was swiftly curtailed when Mother came back early, as she had looked out of the window while she was singing one of the hymns and saw our heads bobbing up and down. Kay was sent home in disgrace and told not to come and play again, even though she was not the instigator, and Joyce and I received a well-deserved scolding. Looking back, I cannot understand why we had been left alone without adult supervision. My parents must have felt that it was more important to 'praise the Lord' than stay at home looking after four bouncy young children.

During the war, my parents were founder members of Union Church along with Marion Harris, the Coxes and the Keeps. Initially, they met in one of their homes, but when enough money was collected, they built a wooden hut diagonally across the road in Northiam. After many years, a brick-built church was built next door with money from a church in the Barbican area of London, which was extensively bombed during the Blitz. Later, a brick-built hall replaced the hut and was used for the Sunday school, brownies, guides, cubs and scouts, the youth club, for various pantomimes, dances and beetle drives, and for Mother's nursery school. Later, Alan and I played badminton there for a few years.

Joyce and I used to have our straight mousy hair cut into a bob with a curtain draped over our forehead and secured with a large bow on the top of one side of our head. We did not look cute; far from it, we looked ridiculous. When I was at junior school, some of the boys took great pleasure in undoing my bow and, quite unfairly, I used to get into no end of trouble when I arrived home. I always wanted to have long hair and look cool with plaits and a fringe like my best friend, Kay, but this was not even considered by my mother, let alone allowed. I can remember hiding behind the curtains once with Joyce and cutting her a far from fetching, rather lopsided fringe. While I was about it, I cut the hair of my antique French 'Jumeau' doll, Barbara, as I was told that she had real hair, so naively I thought that it would grow. It didn't. This was the doll that my maternal granny had been given when she was nine, so I was told that she was rather precious and not the type of doll that you could take to bed to cuddle. I did not even have a teddy, as during and after the war, like everything else, these were either too expensive or in short supply. I used to find comfort in holding on to the thick edge of the blanket and moving my hand along it to send myself to sleep. I would have loved to have had a soft toy to cuddle. My brother, Alan, was fortunate and had a large blue rabbit called 'Bunjy', although it was stuffed with rather uncomfortable wood shavings which later leaked.

Fast forward twenty years to one Christmas, when I made my two nieces, Alison and Anna, and two nephews, Chris and Ian, a large soft toy dog each and stuffed them with kapok. The kapok went everywhere, completely covering the room and most of me, including my nose, hair and eyelashes. I should have worn goggles, a mask and the kind of Personal Protective Equipment (PPE) that health workers are wearing (if they are lucky enough to have it) during the Covid-19 pandemic. My children, Claire and Martin, were very envious and said, 'You make floppy dogs for our cousins, but you don't do it for us,' so I sat up into the night on Christmas Eve and made two more dogs, even being careful to vacuum up the stray kapok to keep my sewing endeavours a secret. When Christmas Day arrived, the children whooped with delight when they saw the wrapped-up shape of two floppy dogs under the Christmas tree. I think that they were their favourite presents, ever. They still have them forty years later!

Much later still, I learned from an article in the *Daily Telegraph* that my antique 'Jumeau' doll was valuable, even with her spikey hair. Barbara had ball-jointed arms and legs, a beautiful bisque face, an unusual open mouth displaying two top teeth, holes in her ears for earrings and now a blonde crew cut. Sadly, I sold her at auction at Sotheby's for £1,500 in 1982 to fund my outrageously expensive divorce, which probably allowed my solicitor to buy his very own tropical island.

At 20 Laurel Way, Christmas was always fun for the family. We had a Christmas tree and decorated it with childish homemade decorations, and we festooned the house with paper chains. Mother always made sure that every picture was adorned with greenery, chiefly holly with a profusion of scarlet berries. On Christmas Eve we placed one of Pop's woollen socks at the foot of the bed and woke up early on Christmas morning to see what Santa had brought us. Every year, there was a satsuma in the toe, a shiny penny, some hazelnuts (ugh), a little notebook and pencil, some boiled sweets, a packet of hair slides, and a cheap toy. For years, we insisted that we 'believed' in Santa until it became ridiculous and this pantomime ended prematurely. We always had our main present-giving in the hallowed front room around the fire after the Queen's Christmas speech on the radio at three o'clock. We had to make lists of the presents that we received so that we could write the dreaded 'thank-you letters' to the correct person. Our letters were scrutinised by Mother to make sure that they were well-written, rather like the way that the letters from boys at boarding schools and correspondence from criminals in confinement were subjected to rigorous checking by the authorities.

Once the present-giving finished, Pop would save every bit of wrapping paper, string and ribbon for next year. He was one of the early recyclers who was ahead of his time and hated throwing anything away. His mantra was: 'It will come in handy.' The paper was smoothed out and meticulously stored somewhere safe in the increasingly over-flowing garage for the coming year. String was a valuable commodity. I think that my son, Martin, has inherited his grandfather's auspicious recycling mentality as he thoughtfully founded the 'The 2 Minute Foundation' charity aimed at encouraging the public to use the litter-picker provided to spend two minutes picking up detritus from beaches and open spaces.

We played a number of indoor games as a family. We played Snakes and Ladders, the age-old board game which was invented in the second century BC; Monopoly, which was introduced in 1935; and Sorry, which was introduced in 1934 and became a family favourite. Monopoly was always rather cut-throat when we displayed our rather combative, competitive natures in a vigorous struggle to win at all costs. I think that Monopoly caused us to be zealously ruthless, rather than encouraging us to display a budding business acumen. Our card games, which included Snap, Rummy, Lexicon and Happy Families, were rather tame in comparison.

We never played Scrabble, even though it was introduced in 1948 and is a game that I am totally hooked on today, as I thoroughly enjoy having friends round to pit my wits against and hopefully make use of my brain cells before they shrivel and die. I find that Super-Scrabble, with its large board and quadruple letters and words, is a brilliant game to play and provides about three hours of humorous entertainment. Would you believe that during this lockdown for Covid-19 you could actually play a game called *Pandemic*! Not a good idea, as it might catch on and become viral…

Mother enjoyed doing the *Daily Telegraph* crossword and I think that I have inherited from her the love of cryptic crosswords. My partner Nick regularly completes the *Daily Telegraph* Toughie, while I struggle each day with the Cryptic and Quick crosswords and, more often or not, need his help.

One year, my father made me a wooden model theatre for Christmas so that I could entertain myself and anyone who was sufficiently patient, or sat still for long enough, to an extremely amateurish show. It had curtains, a backdrop with scenery and actors attached to horizontal wires so that I could push them onto the stage from the wings. I loved it. The model theatre occupied rather a lot of space, so it was kept on the floor in a corner of the dining room. Unfortunately, when I was clearing the dining table one day, I tripped and crashed right onto the new playhouse so that it shattered as if a bomb had achieved a direct hit. I surveyed the damage, then cried and cried and cried some more. Pop mended his masterpiece, but I never felt the same about it again.

One year, my parents were out on Christmas Eve, so Alan and I found the Christmas presents hidden under my parents' bed, which, like all double beds in those days, was high off the ground (so that the chamber pot could be kept underneath), and carefully unwrapped the string from each one to see what we were going to be getting. It was great fun, rather secretive and our parents never knew that we had been peeking. Unfortunately, this meant that Christmas Day was a flop and provided no excitement or surprises but was rather boring, so we never repeated this act of seasonal 'treachery'.

Another year, we went to Auntie Doll's and Uncle Tom's for Christmas Day. For some reason unknown to us, we had to call them auntie and uncle even though they were not related to us or to each other. We were told that Mother's friend, Doll, lived on the ground-floor flat while Tom lived upstairs. We did not believe this arrangement for one moment as they were such a happy unit. Where was her bed? We knew that mother disapproved of people 'living in sin', so perhaps she deluded herself in order to retain their friendship, or maybe they kept their relationship a secret so as not to offend her. As children, we asked repeatedly about their circumstances, but Mother categorically refused to answer our searching questions, which, as you can imagine, made us all the more curious. If this was living in sin, it was to be recommended as it was a very happy relationship. However, as they had no children, they made a big fuss of us and we had one of the most memorable Christmases ever.

Mother had another friend, Auntie Phyllis (yes, we had to call her auntie too!), who lived in a beautiful thatched cottage, yes, with roses round the door, in Kingston Lisle, Oxfordshire. She invited us to stay one summer, so we enjoyed the sounds and the smells of the countryside from the next-door farm and became best buddies with all the animals – well, just the pretty ones. Phyllis was a talented pianist and played the organ for the church next door so was well-known in the village. She lived happily with her friend, Elizabeth, until there was, we were told, 'a falling out'. It was the first time that I realised that two women could live together and have a lesbian relationship.

Auntie Phyllis's period cottage was rather on the small side and was built in the days before bathrooms were considered necessary. The tin bath was to be found under a board which doubled as a working surface in the kitchen. At Auntie Phyllis's, Joyce and I had to share a large antique brass bed. We tried having a bolster between us and also 'top and tailing', but somehow, we always invaded each other's space and were not happy having to share. The bed had round brass knobs at each corner, which we unscrewed and filled with notes to each other. I would love to know if these notes were ever found, and if so, what was written on these childish messages.

At Christmas, our best presents each year came from Auntie Nora, my maternal grandmother's cousin and Mother's godmother, who was not blessed with children and was exceptionally generous to us. She had a room in her large house which was especially given over to storing Christmas and birthday presents. How cool is that? She used to ask us ahead of time what we would like and she would send us anything, provided it was not an umbrella, as she said, 'They were so difficult to pack.' When Joyce and I enjoyed dressmaking, Auntie Nora sent us dress material for Easter, which was a wonderful present and most welcome. This diminutive distant relative lived in an imposing house in the Wirral with her housekeeper and gardener, and my mother can remember that when she was young she would be met at the station rather grandly by a 'coach and four' (a coach and four horses). Auntie Nora was a product of the Victorian age, so, just like Queen Victoria, when her husband died prematurely, she wore black (her widow's weeds) for the rest of her long life.

At home in winter, the three of us were sent into the garden sporting knitted navy-blue zipped-up cat-suits, complete with cosy woolly hoods, the forerunners of the onesies. Mother must have been so proud of her brood (and her knitting), as we must have looked like 'daddy bear', 'mummy bear' and 'baby bear' in the three sizes of our hand-made outfits. Mother enjoyed making our dresses, knitting us jumpers or crocheting our cardigans. When I was a teenager she crocheted me a white cotton mini dress with dark blue flowers at the hem, which was a big hit with the boys as the holes were rather revealing. I later gave it to my daughter Claire, who loved the dress too and commented, 'I have had so many compliments.' I knew just what she meant. We were encouraged to knit, sew and embroider from a very young age and loved learning those practical skills. I made a selection of doll's clothes, even once knitting on pins, actual dressmaking pins, to make a dress for a tiny doll that was only three-inches tall. I still have this miniature example of this crazy childhood skill, as it brings back a raft of fond memories.

Mother altered our dresses as we grew; how I abhorred having hand-me-down clothes, the lot of the youngest child. When we pushed our feet through the well-worn cotton sheets, she would cut them down the centre and stitch 'sides to middle' so we would end up with a seam down the centre of our 'make-do-and-mend' sheets, which was most uncomfortable. Mother had a vintage Singer sewing machine, with a turning handle, which meant that you could only hold and direct the material that you were stitching with one hand. Despite this disadvantage, Joyce and I made a number of clothes for ourselves, always as neat on the inside as the outside. Eventually, I bought an electric sewing machine with a foot pedal, which made life so much easier, as I could steer the material with both hands. This novel machine could reverse stitch to secure the seam and also zig-zag to finish off the edges. With this welcome improvement, we never needed to use the trusty pinking shears ever again.

When I needed to borrow money from my father to buy a sewing machine, tennis racquet or hockey stick, he would willingly give me a loan and then make a note in his diary. Each time I paid a contribution off from my pocket money, he would note down how much there was still owing. It was a good system, which certainly taught me the value of money. Since then, I have never borrowed money and kept to the famous phrase uttered by Polonius in *Hamlet*, 'Neither a borrower or a lender be.'

When Joyce and I were teenagers, we would buy a length of material, a 'Simplicity' or, for special occasions and more money, a 'Vogue' pattern, a reel of cotton and a matching zip, and come home, cut it out and make a short evening dress in a day, then enjoy wearing it the same night. This way we could have the exact colour and design that we wanted. I made my tennis dresses and even made a suede coat using a thick heavy-duty sewing machine needle. Whenever I was cutting out, I remembered the cautionary tale that Mother related to me; apparently, when my maternal grannie was young, she cut out a dress and cut through the tablecloth too!

When I was older, I adored going to shops, which stocked a full range of fabrics. My favourite was John Lewis in Oxford Street, where I would be in seventh heaven and totally spoiled for choice. I bought my white satin wedding dress material and African violet bridesmaid's material from there, plus all the trimmings, and carried the large roll home on the tube. I added white fox fur to the hem of my wedding dress, as a nod to my penchant for fur. Joyce made her own bridesmaid's dress and I made my physio friend Meriel's dress when we were seconded to Banstead Hospital for two weeks. I then made a red suit with large black buttons, 'so Mary Quant', worn with a glorious black fox fur hat for my going-away outfit. Later, I was delighted to be asked to make a bridesmaid dress for Kay's sister, Linda, when Kay was married to Don. What an honour!

Mother never learned to drive, which made life exceedingly difficult for her, so she had a basket on wheels. I can remember at the time thinking that I would not have been seen dead with it, but now I am much older, I would far prefer to push or pull something along than carry it home. She always wore a twin set and a mid-calf tweed skirt. This hid a fine woollen vest enveloped in a professionally fitted pink all-in-one corset with suspenders attached holding up her lisle stockings. She wore voluminous silky pink Ceylonese bloomers, which reached to her knees, with knicker elastic, where she tucked her embroidered linen handkerchief. Her outfit was completed with sensible brown leather lace-up shoes.

I can remember going up to town as a teenager in shiny stiletto winkle-pickers with a four-inch heel, then walking home from Woodside Park station in my stockinged feet, as my shoes were killing me. How daft was that! The vanity of youth. Having said that, I never learned my lesson, because when I went to Buckingham Palace to collect my MBE, the first thing that I did in the taxi going back to the hotel was to throw my killer shoes off! The second thing was to donate them to a charity shop (only worn once by Royal appointment).

I must say now that I am eighty, I am not a follower of the latest fashion but dress for comfort not style. I leave looking cool to my granddaughters, Maggie and Charlie, who look beautiful in any of the latest fashions. Indeed, they would look a million dollars in a bin-liner. I cannot wear high heels anymore, as they hurt the balls of my feet too much, and I am happiest in Skecher's shoes, with their memory-foam insoles, which give me and my elderly joints some sort of shock absorbency. Also, believe it or not, I have taken to wearing hats, not 'when I am old, I will wear purple' ones or going to the Palace finery, but Barbour headgear to avoid getting wet, sunburnt or just windswept. I wear comfortable trousers most days, so that I can get away without wearing tights, and today, now I am cocooned in Ireland, I am wearing my partner Nick's bright pink shorts as it is so hot! My daughter Claire, who is isolated in my house in Devon, has texted me to say that she has made two of my new tea-towels into a pair of shorts and sent me a photograph. I can remember, when I was young and slim, that I made a pair of shorts from a yard of orange sailcloth material. I doubt if I would get one leg in now! Having admitted to that, I am happiest when I undress in the evening and wear a white fluffy dressing gown to relax, read or watch television. Life is good.

When I was young, the local shops were stocked with only basic items for customers, who were content wearing a plain woollen twin set with a grey 'terylene' pleated skirt, the uniform of the smart set. Locally, we shopped at Priors department store in North Finchley, where there was a fascinating overhead system of wires connected from the counter to a cashier sitting in a desk near the ceiling. When the shop assistant took money for a purchase, she placed it in a tube with the price ticket, pulled a lever and sent it whizzing up to the cashier sitting aloft, who then sent the change with a receipt whistling back in the same tube to the customer. As children we were intrigued by this brilliant system and enjoyed waving to the lady sitting impressively 'in the Gods'. Credit cards were unheard of then.

For anything more stylish that was suitable for teenagers, we had to go up to town. My mother loved going to Selfridges and DH Evans (then a subsidiary of Harrods), where she had accounts and where the shop assistants knew her by name. When we went up to the West End as youngsters, Mother made sure that we were suitably dressed in our best coat, beret and white gloves. She also had this ridiculous rule that she would never enter DH Evans carrying a Selfridges bag and vice versa! What a difference from these days, when cash not status is king, and where customers can rock up in any casual gear, the more bizarre the better! Selfridges is now filled with different retail concessions, each with their own branded products, and DH Evans became part of House of Fraser in 2001.

When we were young, as a treat, we were taken to a news theatre in Oxford Street to see some cartoon films (and the news), while Mother rested her legs before taking us to the Lyons Corner House for afternoon tea, where the waitresses (called 'Nippies') wore black alpaca dresses with white collars and cuffs, square white aprons and starched white caps. They served us delicious cream pastries, quite unlike anything that we had at home. Sadly, these once-popular tea shops closed in 1981.

Each year in November, Mother took us to the Mowbray Religious Bookshop in Piccadilly, where she bought her Christmas cards. She would only purchase religious cards, as she considered that it was unchristian to send a card that featured anything other than a nativity scene. I can remember buying children's Christmas cards there with outlines for colouring in. To date, Nick and I have sent cards which contain wild animals such as foxes, stags, squirrels and rabbits, believing that they are just as Christmassy.

We had a number of family outings, educational and otherwise. I can clearly remember being taken to the circus and seeing pretty, scantily clad girls standing on white horses and balancing precariously while they cantered round the ring, often jumping nimbly from one steed to another without slipping off.

I never liked the clowns, not because I had coulrophobia, but because I thought, even as a child, that their slapstick humour was seriously unfunny. I was thrilled to see the trapeze artists high up in the roof of the big top flying from one trapeze to another and performing all sorts of risky manoeuvres, without so much as a climbing rope or a safety net. I loved seeing the elephants arrive trunk to tail, but I was frightened when I saw a trainer enter the cage with the lions and brutally use a whip to make these frightened large cats sit on drums. As a child, I thought it was cruel to keep wild animals in a cage and even worse to threaten them with a leather lash. I could imagine how the trainers must have trained these wild animals and it wasn't pretty. Fortunately, animal welfare groups have at last succeeded in lobbying the government to ban the use of wild animals in circuses in England, but would you believe that the Wild Animals Circuses Act did not become law until 2019?

Talking of wild animals in cages, we did enjoy our visits to both London and Whipsnade Zoo. As a child, I was amazed by the height of the giraffes, the size of the galumphing elephants and the surprising sight of seeing tigers sitting in water looking rather pleased with themselves without a care in the world. I was extremely unhappy to see a polar bear pacing backwards and forwards across an inadequate cage in a one-bear protest to being cruelly confined to a cell. He was obviously exceedingly disturbed at being restricted. In contrast, I loved seeing the streamline penguins move seamlessly both in and out of the water, and I must admit that I laughed heartily along with the chimpanzees at their tea party.

Now, that I am an adult, I am ambivalent about zoos keeping wild and exotic animals in captivity. In support of zoos, I am told that the breeding programmes keep the endangered species alive; I realise that the animal habitats have been expanded considerably, that keepers are much more knowledgeable and caring and keep the animals occupied, and I know that it is the only opportunity for many adults and children to be educated and see a range of animals from the wild. The gate money allows zoos to care for animal orphans and those unfortunate injured creatures who may otherwise be unable to survive. Conversely, animals in captivity suffer from boredom, stress and confinement (in much the same way as humans do in isolation from Covid-19!); animals can plot their escape and sometimes be successful making the population at risk; and finally, not all breeding programmes are able to release the animals back into the wild. To add to this dichotomy, people receive a vast amount of novel education and insight into animals in their natural world from the amazing array of wildlife programmes on television. David Attenborough is my hero and, together with his vast team of cameramen with their roving cameras, has brought the exotic animals into my living room. Thank you, David. Should we not be satisfied with that?

Later in my life, I was fortunate to go on safari to the Kruger National Park, and by far the best experience, even more surreal than viewing the elephants, lions, rhinos and giraffes, was seeing a mother cheetah with four gorgeous cubs sitting together in the long grass, each cute little face marked with distinctive black tear marks. This snapshot of family life in the wild had to be among my best-ever sightings of animal life. I know the young of all animals is appealing, but these cubs were beyond beautiful, truly exquisite. Having extolled the virtues of visiting a wildlife park, when I was in Australia I was lucky enough to hug a koala. Possibly, I should not have handled a wild animal, who weighed more than I would have thought (how can you become that heavy with just a diet of eucalyptus leaves?), as it is now illegal to cuddle a koala in Victoria or New South Wales, as they say that it causes them stress, but I must say in my defence that the beloved koala hugged me back.

In 1951, when Joyce was just twelve and I was ten and a half, we were allowed to go together, without an adult, to the Festival of Britain on the South Bank, a fair which was aimed at promoting industry, arts and science for a 'better Britain'. We saw the 'Skylon', a spectacular cigar-shaped steel structure, which had the illusion of floating above the ground and was, sadly, removed when the exhibition was dismantled in 1952. Why? Apparently, the £30,000 cost of dismantling and re-erecting this novel construction elsewhere was deemed too much for a government struggling with post-war austerity. There is a model of Skylon, designed by Moya, Powell and Samuely at the Museum of London, which is near St Paul's Cathedral. My most vivid memory of the festival was entering the Dome of Discovery and seeing screens showing the many developmental stages of a baby in the womb prior to parturition. As a young girl, I was completely enthralled with these images, which sparked my interest in human anatomy and obstetrics.

I certainly did not know then that I would become a physiotherapist specialising in the pelvic floor and all the complications that could come from the trauma of giving birth. In this capacity, I have treated patients who have had torn pelvic floor muscles, prolapses, urinary incontinence and, most devastating of all, faecal incontinence. Fortunately, most of these conditions can be helped by a course of pelvic floor exercises and the correct advice. I loved helping these young women after their birth injuries and, much later, was pleased to share my knowledge when I lectured about the female pelvic floor muscles to physiotherapists in many countries around the world. My parents would have been thrilled that I was teaching!

Pop enjoyed teaching us too. He made sure that we were shown the rudiments of carpentry, so that we could use a hammer, wield a saw and drive a chisel with precision. I never use a knife now without hearing Pop say, 'Never cut towards yourself?' I loved being with Pop in the garage and was delighted to be able to make a jewellery box, complete with dove-tail joints, with his help. This reminds me of a friend who decided to make a doll's house for his young daughter, who happened to wander into the garage while he was working. 'What are you making?' she asked, so he thought quickly and said, 'I am making a chest of drawers,' to which she replied, 'If you don't want it as a chest of drawers, it would make a lovely doll's house.'

Pop was happiest in the garage with all his and his father's tools to hand. He descended into a pit to service the trusty Standard 10 car, usually the night before we went on holiday. It never broke down, but was once caught in a flood, so we children refused to travel in it for quite a while as the smell was overwhelmingly grim. There was no heater in the car, so in winter Mother had a sheepskin foot-muff and car rug while her offspring froze in the back. There were no seatbelts, but it did sport hilarious flap, up and down, illuminated indicators, which at the time seemed modern as they obviated the need for mechanically winding down the window to give well-intentioned hand signals. There was a chrome and yellow metal AA badge perched on the front bumper and Father (and naturally we children too) always saluted when we saw the AA man in his brown uniform coming towards us on his motorcycle and yellow sidecar. Later, as more cars arrived on the roads, the AA men were relieved of saluting, so long journeys lost their appeal. It was boring to go on long-distance car journeys and too bumpy to read, so we devised a series of games such as 'I-spy' and 'the first person to see a car of a certain colour?', culminating in the age-old hackneyed question, 'the first person to see the sea?' There were no iPads or Kindles then, no car radios and certainly no music from wireless Bluetooth headphones. The renowned *I-Spy* books were not launched until 1992, so it was no surprise that we teased each other, often quite physically, in the back of the car and were often reprimanded.

There were no car seats when we were babies, no booster seats as we grew and seatbelts were unknown. Fortunately, to date, great progress has been made in motor car design to include reversing lights, indicator lights, heaters, air-conditioning, demisters, power steering, seatbelts, air bags, electric windows, automatic windscreen wipers and, best of all, satellite navigation. In the UK, postcodes have helped visitors and delivery men with satnavs to find the right address, though sometimes difficulties arise as a number of houses share the same postcode. In Ireland, the system arrived later and is therefore more advanced, so the Eircodes are unique for each dwelling, making it a whole lot easier to find the right property.

We *always* went on holiday to a cheap guest house in Eastbourne down a side road from the sea. One year, Joyce and I became lost, and it took us ages to find the unidentifiable building as each road was filled with a row of similar Regency-style houses. The owner of the guest house cruelly turfed us out after breakfast and we were not allowed to return until dinner time. In those post-war years, we were each allocated a glass of sugar to last the week, but Pop kindly swapped some of our tea rations with the other guests for extra sugar. Dinner was frugal: there was a choice of tomato soup, brown Windsor soup or orange squash (not juice) as a starter, followed by a matchbox-sized portion of meat (usually Spam), potatoes and one vegetable (often tinned). The dessert was equally unexciting and could be either spotted dick and custard or some ghastly slithery milk pudding such as tapioca (frogspawn) or sago. You can see why we needed the sugar!

I can remember the day in 1953 when sweet rationing ended. We queued up outside a confectionary shop in Eastbourne and were allowed to have whatever we could afford. Previously, we had only been able to buy eight ounces of sweets or chocolate a month.

I was five years old in 1945, when the first Fyffe banana boat since the Second World War docked in Avonmouth, bringing a consignment of ten million bananas. Alan, Joyce and I had never seen a banana before, and Mother bought some for us as a special treat. We took an immediate dislike to the unexpected taste, much to Mother's surprise and obvious disappointment. Children can be so ungrateful.

In those days, Eastbourne, being a resort for the well-to-do, was filled with women in fur coats (even in summer!), all of whom seemed to own Pekinese dogs, which were popular at the time. As a child I liked the feel of fur (still do) and loved stroking both the coats and the dogs. Mother stopped me from doing this by saying that these furry creatures would bite. I suppose she meant the dogs. I think this was the start of my fur fetish, as even to this day, I am totally unable to pass any fur in a shop without stroking it to see if it is real or fake. I know it is political, but I love the feel of real fur, dead or alive.

Talking of fur, a furry black and white cat came into our garden in Laurel Way while I was picking strawberries in the greenhouse. I tried a few names out on him and discovered that he came to me when I called, 'Picky.' I made a gargantuan fuss of him and he followed me about. The long and the short of it was that we gave Picky food and milk and somewhere to sleep, thus, to all intents and purpose, we adopted him. Looking back, this was irresponsible behaviour, as he might have been someone's much-loved pet. We made no attempt to put a 'FOUND' notice on a lamp-post and trace his owner, as we should have done, had we been kind and thoughtful citizens. In those days, pets were not micro-chipped. Picky lived with us for years and was by far the most popular member of our family. He was very tolerant when I dressed him up in doll's clothes, took him out in my doll's pram or in the basket on the front of my bicycle. He would follow me up the road past six houses to the postbox and when I had posted a letter, he would dash home through everyone's front gardens. I loved him. When we went on holiday, our kind next-door neighbour fed Picky for us, while we fed their marmalade moggy when they went away.

While on holiday at Eastbourne, I can remember sitting on a pebbly beach with the family, often chilled by the wind. Walking to the sea was so uncomfortable for our tender young feet and we couldn't understand why we didn't get taken to a resort with a sandy beach. There were no such things as flip-flops then, as they only became popular in the 1960s, and jelly sandals only became popular in the eighties. Mother had prepared for our holiday by busily knitting navy-blue swimsuits for us. These homemade costumes filled with water and sagged embarrassingly when we emerged from the sea, so we had to wring them out and pull them up over our flat chests before we struggled manfully up the beach, bent double like badly hunched nonagenarians. Sad as it sounds, on wet days we sat under the pier. Although this sounds rather ungrateful, we did enjoy swimming in the sea, and one year we made friends with a boy who had a rubber dinghy and thoroughly enjoyed playing with him in his boat. Looking back, rubber dinghies can float out to sea and spark air-sea rescues, but as a family we were totally unaware of the danger back then.

We enjoyed paying an old penny or two to sit on the pebbles and watch the Punch and Judy show. This traditional puppet show arrived in England from Italy in 1662 and as young children we were spellbound, though I thought that Punch was rather a bully.

We also took bracing walks along the promenade from the pier to the bandstand to see the famous Carpet Gardens with their spectacular fountains and vibrant floral displays. As we passed The Grand Hotel, I dreamed of being able to stay there, as the hotel had facilities for children, such as a swimming pool and table-tennis table. Sixty years later, I gave a lecture at this luxury hotel and commenced my lecture by saying, 'I have always wanted to come to The Grand since I was a child, when we stayed every year at a boarding house down a side street, so thank you for giving me this opportunity to realise my dream.'

We went by car to Beachy Head to look down at the red and white-striped lighthouse constructed in 1902 to a height of forty-three metres but dwarfed by the high white chalk cliffs. We kept well away from the edge of the cliffs, as we were told that the edge could crumble at any moment. The light was electrified in 1920, automated and de-manned in 1983, and eventually converted to solar power in 2011.

We enjoyed going on the pier, even though we were at times buffeted by the wind, and bravely walked three hundred metres to the end. In the forties and fifties, the ladies' toilet needed an old penny in a slot in the door before it would open, leading to the phrase 'to spend a penny'. Later, when there was a price increase to two pence, women still talked about 'spending a penny', possibly because the expression 'lost your tuppence' meant losing your virginity, as in some areas girls' genitalia were called their 'tuppence'. Eastbourne pier was completed in 1872 and was built on stilts resting on cups on the seabed, which allowed the structure to move in bad weather. During the Second World War, the decking was removed to host machine guns to protect the nation, but unluckily a mine exploded and caused considerable damage to the pier itself. It was rebuilt and housed a theatre, which was subsequently destroyed in a fire in 1970, and also ice-cream stalls, penny machines and many benches on the open deck for visitors to enjoy the sunshine, seagulls and squalls of insouciant pier living. Like all children, we loved being treated to ice-cream cornets or wafers.

In Eastbourne, there was a bandstand where young visitors were encouraged to perform to an almost exclusively family audience. One day, with ill-advised bravery and certainly no rehearsal whatsoever, Joyce and I sang and danced in a way that would make your toes curl. Needless to say, we weren't discovered by any national or even local talent-scouts, so we never repeated this embarrassing performance. Never. Ever. Ever.

As a family outing, we were taken to a large sloping green in Hampden Park which sported a selection of old tricycles and bath chairs, with two large wheels at the back and one steering wheel at the front, on which children were allowed to play. We had never seen these antiquated contraptions before, as in the days of my youth, invalids were usually kept indoors. Indeed, if they did venture out, there were no facilities such as slopes and precious few lifts for the disabled. As you can imagine, this activity, which was free, provided a good deal of amusement for the three of us, as we pushed each other around pretending to be elderly invalids. There was no thought then that I would have a career caring for the disabled. Then, we were young and wrapped up in our own carefree existence.

As both my parents were teachers, they had long summer holidays, so Pop took us camping. He attached a homemade trailer, painted a fetching shade of grey to match the Standard 10, and we set off at close to walking speed. The first stop was Salisbury, as Pop wanted to sketch the cathedral. Pop had a Brownie box camera, which he allowed me to use, and although I was keen to take a photograph, I was totally unable to see anything through the cloudy 'one centimetre by one and a half centimetres' viewfinder. I was poised to take a photograph, but I could see nothing at all. Zilch. Oh dear. Eventually, I pointed the camera in the direction of the cathedral and bravely took the shot. Then, I had to wait for the reel to be finished and taken into the chemist to be developed. When I saw my first-ever photograph, I was amazed; it was a miracle, so I put it in for a photography competition, where it won first prize in my age group. I was obviously on my way to becoming a renowned photographer. David Bailey, eat your heart out. Dear reader, I must add that I have never ever taken a photo since which has excited me so much. Now, box cameras are just collector's pieces, which have been superseded by the brilliant cameras on smartphones for most amateurs like me.

When we arrived in Devon, we had to put up the tents on the campsite. We erected one ridge tent for my parents and one for Joyce and me, while Alan had a small Bivvy tent. I loved using the mallet to secure the tent pegs and hammer them into the often unwieldly ground in order to secure the guy ropes. We visited Croyde, Lynton, Lymouth and importantly Ilfracombe, where my parents had spent their honeymoon in 1937. I was encouraged by Mother to make a diary of my holiday to take to school, like a goody-goody, which I still have to this day. It would not win any competitions, but it gave me a brilliant reminder of exactly where we had been.

Another time, we visited North Wales and walked around Betws-y-Coed and admired its beauty before all the kiss-me-quick shops arrived and spoiled its natural setting. We visited Portmeirion, which was built in the style of a stunning Italian village by Sir Clough Williams-Ellis from 1925 to 1976, and found it to be like a film set. Each little house was unique, each clinging to the hillside precariously, each pleasantly painted from a pastel palette. It is now a top tourists' destination and a cracking place to stay for a holiday overlooking the sea or, for the favoured few, a top wedding venue. Then, we went to Snowdon and walked up until my young legs 'went', so Mother took me up on the train while the rest of the family climbed nobly to the top. I was never good at walking up hills and only wish that all hills had a similar mode of transport as an alternative to walking.

I alternated between being indolent and being madly energetic. I can remember being taken to visit my maternal grandfather in hospital with angina and only being interested in eating his or his neighbour's grapes. We never had grapes at home, so this was a luxury. When I was taken to visit Great Auntie Hetty, who was bed-bound in hospital with rheumatoid arthritis, I thought how lovely it must be to stay in bed all the time and have your meals brought to you. And to think that I, a young sloth, would become a physiotherapist and spend a lifetime encouraging patients to move! Nowadays, cortisone and physiotherapy are recommended for patients with rheumatoid arthritis.

I visited my maternal grandmother when she was very ill with pneumonia. Many years previously, she had inhaled a tooth when she was at the dentist, which led to a number of lung abscesses and attendant chest problems. I made sure that my lovely dentist was conversant with this story before he extracted one of my teeth! Thinking about it after the event, I am sure that it was ill-advised to tell him this, as it probably made him even more jittery than I was. When we were very young, we were given a boiled sweet after a visit to the dentist, presumably meant to rot our young teeth, increase the cavities and drum up trade!

Each year, we were taken to the pantomime at the Golders Green Hippodrome, which produced a very professional performance, and when Alan joined the cubs we enjoyed seeing the Scout 'Gang Show' there. As a treat, we were taken to Golders Green to see *Lilac Time*, a musical designed for wholesome family entertainment. I loved seeing the performers in their colourful old-fashioned outfits against the amazingly creative scenery, all the while hearing the lilting singing to music composed by Schubert. I was particularly thrilled to see the ladies in their revealing low-cut dresses take a final bow and display their ample bosoms. I hoped that one day I would have bouncing boobs and a cleavage of my own.

One year, Joyce was invited to go to the opera, but I was not invited because I was told that I would be too fidgety! However, after much protest, I was taken to the ballet to see *Swan Lake*.

I was mesmerised; I was totally transfixed; it was me on the stage in a tutu dancing to the dreamy music of Tchaikovsky surrounded by all the beautiful dancers in the chorus; I was totally absorbed in this magical production; I did not want it to end. I was entranced. Could I sit still? You bet. I didn't move.

When the three of us graduated from Mrs Blundell's 'Academy' we were sent to Totteridge Primary School. The only thing that I can remember there was when a boy in my form proudly showed his willy to the rest of the astounded class. He was gently told, 'Put it away,' by the open-mouthed schoolmistress, and he tucked it temporarily out of sight. However, the next day, it was out again when he peed into a dear little girl's Wellington boot. On the third day and every day thereafter, he was absent from class, having been expelled at the tender age of five years. I wonder what happened to him and how he ended up? I bet this expulsion was missing when he cobbled together his CV.

I don't think the juvenile exposure or the 'bootie' had anything to do with my parents' decision to take us away from the 'school on the green'. My parents were more interested in our progress, or lack of it, so they decided that Church Hill Road Junior School in East Barnet was a vast improvement educationally. We had walked to Totteridge school by taking a short-cut through Coppice Walk, which was rather scary in case we bumped into any strange men. It was instilled in us not to talk to strangers or accept lifts from them, which meant that any unknown man was immediately under suspicion. I can clearly remember when I was walking home once that a car stopped and a man offered me a lift. As he was a stranger, I declined the offer. Later that day, Mother made fun of me, because it was someone from church whom she felt that I ought to have known. As a child, I felt that I ought to have been praised for being sensible, not ridiculed for trying to keep myself safe. It is extraordinary how I have remembered this injustice more than seventy years later.

Chapter 3

Junior School

Church Hill Road Junior School in East Barnet was further away. I had to walk up to the High Road and catch a 125 bus to school. I stood at the bus stop and shivered in winter. Mother declared that I couldn't have fur-lined boots as these were 'common', so instead I had a severe case of chilblains, which itched every time they became warm. I was taken to the doctor, who gave me some pills to increase my circulation which made my toes tingle, but they failed to help. I used to squash my toes under the footrest of my school desk to numb them, so I could concentrate in class. I told my mother this, but still there were no bloody boots.

In the winter, Joyce and I were made to wear a liberty bodice over our fine woollen 'Chilprufe' vest. I always thought that this was an austerity garment cobbled together to keep the young warm in the post-war years, but no, liberty bodices were invented at the end of the nineteenth century in order to liberate women from their previously heavily boned and firmly laced corsets. Boneless, laceless or not, this unwelcome undergarment was hideous. It consisted of a sleeveless bodice made from white fleecy fabric with re-enforcing cotton tapes, rubber buttons down the front and similar buttons for suspenders at the side. I hated it. When I changed for games at junior school, I noticed that the other children just wore vests. I was different: I was the child wearing a liberty bodice. When Mother gave me mine I used to recite, 'Liberty-iberty-ib, liberty-iberty-ib, liberty bodices, liberty bodices, liberty-iberty-ib,' and pull a face so anguished that it could cut through concrete. To complete this thoroughly unattractive look, I wore the ubiquitous navy-blue knickers and white socks. Thus, I went to school with a warm chest, cold knees and icy toes.

There was a conductor on the bus who took our children's tickets from a ticket holder and when we paid, he punched holes in them from a metal punching device that he wore strapped to his chest. These old-fashioned devices are now in the London Bus Museum in Weybridge or available on eBay. Some conductors disliked children, but one particular man whom we named 'Smiley' was happy to see us, so we always loved getting onto his bus. When we reached our stop, we had to ring the red bell and then run down the hill to the school.

One rainy day, an elderly gentleman closed his umbrella and alighted our bus, but I noticed that after a short while, his umbrella started to steam, or was it smoke? When he left the bus at the stop before mine, he unfurled his brolly, which showed that there was a gaping hole in the material. He was totally unaware of the loss of protection and went merrily on his way with his holey umbrella held above him. Bless him. I can remember wanting to care for this elderly man. Was I, for the first time, showing empathy for my fellow man, a trait that I gradually developed when I became a physiotherapist?

I was only late for school once, when the bus failed to

turn up. Unfortunately, it was the day that the headmaster was ready to present me at assembly with a certificate for winning a National Handwriting Competition. He was furious when I arrived late. I felt that this was most unfair, as I should have been congratulated not reprimanded. Still do. I had perfected a classical script with a pen dipped into ink and was able to write accurately without trembling. This all changed when I went to grammar school and they made us change our writing style to speed-writing. Now, I am ashamed of my writing as it looks very wobbly and most unattractive. My father wrote in this preferable copper-plate style to the day he died at the age of ninety.

I had three friends at school, who all lived in East Barnet, so it was difficult to socialise with them out of school. They went to all the latest films and I felt that I had missed out, when they were discussing them in great detail. In needlework, the four of us made short circular skirts with matching boleros. We wore these when we performed an acrobatic display to the school at the end of term, which finished with me standing on the shoulders of one of the taller girls. I shudder now to think how dangerous this must have been, but I had the ignorance (and balance) that comes with youth.

My friends and I were very active, and we found that we could swing on the overhead pipes in the girls' lavatories. It is a wonder that these did not burst; however, before this could happen some killjoy must have split on us, because we were reprimanded and all lined up in the hall for the cane. We stood with our hands out waiting for our punishment, but in the end, we were let off with a scolding and the type of memory which produces vivid nightmares in perturbed and anxious children.

My friends at school told me the facts of life and I can clearly remember thinking that my mother should have told me, so like a horrible child, I decided to put her on the spot. We were walking down the hill back home once and I said to my mother: 'What are those bins for in the public lavatories?' My mother whispered, 'I can't tell you now, but I will tell you when we get home.' When we arrived home, she ushered me into the front room, the room reserved for guests, the room where we were allowed to toast crumpets over the open fire, the room that was only used for special occasions. This was the room that she chose to tell me about the birds and the bees. With much stuttering and stumbling, she started to enlighten me about periods, pregnancy and babies. There was no mention of love, sperm or the delights of intercourse. Poor Mother, she was clearly embarrassed. I felt for her. Today, there are some excellent books on the market which would have explained the facts of life in much more detail, but then I had to make do with Mother's staggeringly self-conscious performance. This was a very different side to Mother's personality, as usually, she was confident and dictatorial. I always believed that she was controlling because she was a teacher, who stood no nonsense from her pupils, and that this rubbed off on the way that she controlled her family.

Looking back, I realise that she never hugged me or told me that she loved me but seemed hell-bent on making sure that I was brought up properly. A kind of Victorian approach. She certainly instilled a sense of right or wrong in me, but also an irrational fear of being constantly reprimanded. My friends seemed to have a much warmer and more loving relationship with their mothers. I was particularly fond of Kay's mother and would have loved to have moved in with her.

I am stretching my memory but cannot remember any specific birthday party that we had at home. Our house was not big enough for children to run around, so we commandeered the church hut for our parties. We mostly had homemade party dresses, though occasionally, we had expensive dresses that Auntie Nora had kindly sent to us. I know that we played party games such as 'Grandmother's footsteps', 'we all pat the dog', 'musical chairs', 'musical bumps', 'pin the tail on the donkey' and, most popular of all, 'passing the parcel', particularly if you were the birthday girl and the adults stopped the music at the right time. There were always sandwiches, orange or lemon squash, jelly and ice-cream, and a birthday cake, but there were no take-home presents for the little guests in those days.

We never had 'Prom parties' or celebrated eighteenth birthdays like today's teenagers; the big birthday was the coming-of-age at twenty-one. I can vividly remember celebrating my twenty-first birthday wearing a strapless midnight-blue dress, matching the sapphire in my new engagement ring that Tony had kindly given me. I invited forty friends to a dance in the church hall, to the music from a lively three-piece band. Much, much later, I held a party at home in Chesham Bois for all the family to celebrate my mother's seventieth birthday. She was most grateful and said that it was the first birthday party that she had ever had. How achingly sad was that.

While I was growing up, my mother had certain weird ideas which I was not allowed to correct or criticise. She gave me a watch that kept stopping and said that this was because I had so much electricity in me. Can you believe it! She wouldn't countenance the fact that the watch could have been faulty. It was. When a friend asked if I would like to ride her pony, Mother said that I wouldn't be able to ride as you need to turn your feet in when horse-riding, whereas you are trained to turn your feet out for ballet. There was no merit in letting her know that you could do both. My feet turned whichever way I wanted them to turn, for goodness' sake.

Mother disapproved of women who did not wear corsets, those who 'let themselves go'. When I developed a figure, she bought me a roll-on complete with two front and two side suspenders which gave me stomach cramp, when I was in the cinema, so I took this restrictive garment off and hoped that my stockings would not fall down. My roll-on was swiftly replaced with a suspender belt, which was infinitely more comfortable and kept my stockings in place, though it was always tricky to keep the back seam perfectly straight. It was not until the 1970s that tights became more popular than nylon stockings and women were free from suspenders. More importantly, tights did not have back seams which would twist.

Mother believed that everyone should be able to speak the Queen's English; I cringed when she said that she spoke better than my father, as I thought that she shouldn't voice such a cruel 'put-down', but I kept my thoughts to myself to avoid any uncomfortable argument, which would make the situation considerably worse. I swiftly learned that it was better to ignore throw-away remarks, rather than inflame the situation. Then, strangely, she insisted that I should have elocution lessons. I went to the first lesson as instructed, and as it was such a painful experience, I absolutely refused to continue. I think this was the first time that I had defied my mother.

Joyce and I were both given piano lessons and expected to practise for a short while each day. Joyce became an accomplished pianist, but I fell short of her standards, so I gave up having lessons as I was unable to compete with her. I was never put in for piano exams, funny that, as I did try my best, but sadly it was not to be. I was always told that I 'thumped' the keys; now I pound the keyboard of the computer instead and can use every finger when typing, which I guess is a throw-back from the manual dexterity I learned playing 'Fur Elise' and the 'English Country Garden' until the family begged me to stop. Thus, I rejected any ideas of becoming a renowned concert pianist, for which everybody must be thankful, and while I am on the subject, I rejected any idea of a vocal career, operatic or otherwise, as I was told that I couldn't sing in tune either!

Alan learned the oboe to help with his breathing, as he regularly suffered from bouts of asthma. He mastered the oboe and regularly plays enthusiastically in an orchestra today. I can remember when I was training to be a physiotherapist seeing him in his room during an asthma attack gasping for breath and helping by encouraging him to breathe out, so that he could breathe in more oxygenated air afterwards. It helped if I squeezed the sides of his chest, to help him to exhale. Now, I wonder if the asthma he experienced as a teenager was linked to his hobby of model plane-making. He used to sit in his room for hours studiously putting small pieces of balsa aircraft together using a copious amount of glue, until Mother bustled in and threw the windows open. We now know that sniffing glue can cause a temporary sense of euphoria and, even more worrying, it can impair one's ability to breathe and can lead to chronic respiratory failure, a condition in which the body is unable to take in enough oxygen over time. However, this side effect of glue inhalation was totally unknown then.

Mother thought that certain East End delights such as jellied eels, potted shrimps, cockles and winkles were 'common'. She thought that it was 'common' to wear nail varnish like the beautiful lady who lived next door. She thought one of our neighbours was a 'wicked woman' because she was not married to the man that she lived with. What would she think of my thirty-five-year relationship with Nick? I would like to think that she would have moved with the times. I could never tell her that Tony and I were going to be divorced. She would never have been able to cope with the stigma. What would she say to the people at church? I can remember clearly her saying, when Tony and I got married, 'If anything goes wrong, don't come home,' and when things went pear-shaped this was imprinted in my memory, but, would you believe it, she was a voluntary marriage guidance counsellor! Mother was very keen for us to fly the nest and even offered us an incentive. The first child to leave was to be given Pop's oil painting of bluebells, the one that was submitted to the Royal Academy of Art for the Summer Exhibition but failed at the last hurdle. As I was the first to get married, I have Pop's beautiful painting in my cottage in Devon.

Mother delighted in telling us at mealtimes when young girls from the area had 'fallen' and how they were sent to a home in the country, where their baby would be adopted. I am sure that this information was aimed at letting us know, in no uncertain terms, what would happen to us if we were 'up the duff'. In those days, there was no consideration for the mental health of the frightened young mother or for the future feelings of the innocent baby, who would often not know their biological mother or how to trace them. In those days, mothers of 'the fallen' would agree to give away their grandchild, rather than face the stigma from an uncaring society. I felt that Christians ought to have been more forgiving and caring and be prepared to set an example, but I kept silent for fear of causing an almighty scene. Now that I have matured, I would stand up for what I believe to be in the best interests of the people concerned, from a humane and more compassionate point of view.

One day, out of the blue, Pop brought me home a second-hand red portable gramophone. It had a handle to wind-up before any record was played, about four vinyl seventy-eight-inch records and a few large silver gramophone needles. I can remember that I played 'The Man in the Moon' so many times that the whole family threatened to throw my precious record out of the window. I admit that the sound output was rather scratchy, but it didn't stop me from playing the records repeatedly until they became even scratchier, as I did not have enough pocket money to buy more up-to-date records. To the strains of one of these records, I taught Alan how to waltz in the tight confines of the dining room, but he gave up before his dancing lessons were complete, as his wonderful wife, Rosemary, will testify!

I usually came second in class, so had to share a wooden double-desk with Roger Osbourne, the lad who always came first, though we were told that it would be more competitive when we reached senior school. It was. Most of my friends were rewarded if they passed exams and were offered presents such as bicycles, roller-skates, money or new clothes, if they passed the eleven-plus. My parents failed to offer the three of us any incentives; we were *expected* to do our best. Mother would go through my end-of-term report and say how disappointed she was that I 'talked too much in class' or 'could have tried harder'. Oh dear. I hated bringing my school report home and dreaded the impending post-mortem, one subject at a time. I believe that the teachers (and my parents) should have congratulated me for my good work and ignored the bad and thus encouraged me to thrive. They must have been able to find something positive, for goodness' sake, like my aptitude for sport.

At home, we were given every opportunity to improve educationally. My father brought us home a second-hand set of the *Encyclopaedia Britannica*, so we could look up anything that we needed to know. The main drawback of these books was that they needed updating every so often and ours never were; in fact, they were out of date when they arrived. How lucky children are today, having the internet to refer to, so that they can access up-to-date information concerning just about anything with the tap of a keyboard. Having said that, there is too much information for some schoolwork projects, so students need to have the ability to sift through the data, hone down the facts and confine themselves to the salient points.

At home, we were not bought comics, as they were frowned upon, but instead we received the *Children's Newspaper*, a weekly paper aimed at pre-teenage children to keep them conversant with world news and science. In those days, there were no photographs in newspapers until much later. So instead of having the *Beano*, *Eagle* or *The Dandy*, we fought each other as to who was going to read the *Children's Newspaper* first!

In 1950, Joyce and I were allowed to have the *School Friend*, which was a tame weekly magazine aimed at the pre- to early-teen market. When you became a member, you were given a delightful School Friend Birthday Club badge of a beautiful blue enamel dove facing right with its wings spread upwards sitting on the bronze initials S.F.B.C. I cannot remember what happened to my badge, but these nostalgic old badges are available on the web for £15.

At school, Roger partnered me when we did country dancing, such as 'The Gay Gordons', the 'Eightsome Reel' or 'Strip the Willow' in the school hall to the tune of a gravelly record player, which was contained in a large brown piece of furniture on wheels. I far preferred an older boy, John Pack, who was in the year above, and I can remember playing weddings with him during playtime. I was a nine-year-old bride. My groom was a strapping ten.

Interestingly, when I look back, it was in 1949, when I was nine, that Nick, my current partner, was born! Yes, he is much younger than me, so I am careful not to discuss the war or the grim post-war years. He knows nothing about thriftiness, frugality or food rationing – or even the delights of Spam! Nick likes to cook using the best ingredients sourced from a selection of specialist shops – a far cry from the days of my youth. I am happy to let him take over in the kitchen, as my cooking has been likened to the culinary efforts of Wendy Craig in the television series *Butterflies*, written by the talented Carla Lane and first broadcast in 1978. Much later, when I produced pizza for the family, I said, 'I'll have the burnt one,' to which my son, Martin, replied, 'Mum, they're *all* black.' Today, Nick and I have been together for an amazing thirty-five years and continue to enjoy a cherished relationship.

At school, in the morning's break, we had free milk in a small glass bottle which had a cardboard top with a hole punched in the centre for the paper straw. I hated this milk, particularly when I sucked up the cream at the end. However, one good thing was that two cardboard tops could be placed together and used as the template to make a woollen bobble.

In 1952, I was in the top year at junior school, when we were told by Mr Carter, my favourite teacher, the sad news that King George VI had died and Queen Elizabeth II had acceded to the throne. I can remember that one of the girls in the class cried and needed to be consoled. We had to get used to singing, 'God save our gracious Queen' instead of 'God save our gracious King', which was a struggle. In 1953, I was invited to watch the Coronation on television at Kay's house, as we did not own a set at home. We all gathered round a large piece of highly polished brown furniture sporting a small convex green screen at the top, which needed ages to warm up. There, I saw in black and white, the exquisite gold state coach drawn by eight white horses, the crowds lining the route and, once crowned, the procession out of Westminster Abbey with Her Majesty wearing the magnificent St Edward's crown weighing almost five pounds, on the arm of the Duke of Edinburgh. It is incredible that this was the first time that I had seen television. BBC was the only channel then, as it was not till 1955 that ITV was introduced with its annoying advertisements. Later, we rented a black and white television in case the expensive tube imploded and eventually updated it to a colour set. Now, it is amazing to see the clear colours of today's large high-definition screens and to be astounded by the number of available channels. Now, I hear that we are in the age of streaming, so that families can access Netflix, DVD viewing, catch-up and play box sets, providing that they have a child of twelve to connect it for them!

When I was taken to the cinema, I never liked films in black and white, and my whole world changed when glorious technicolour films were released, even though they were often still accompanied by a colourless second feature film. One of the first colour films we saw was *Bambi*, which made Joyce unhappy when his mother was killed, so we left the cinema early, thus stunting my education, as I never ever saw the ending. My dream was to stay sitting in the cinema and see the film around again, but this was not to be.

At the end of the school day, a pupil was given the privilege of ringing the large school bell to herald going-home time. I can clearly remember the day when my turn came around, and I proudly and loudly rang the bell. Later, when my parents retired to Dorset, Mother used to ring a large handbell to call Pop in from their extensive garden at mealtimes.

In winter, I particularly disliked coming home on my own in the dark and was scared, when I saw a man coming out of the gloom. I would cross over the road and shout: 'Daddy, I'm coming.' Not the best retort to make to a potential paedophile! However, one summer day the young postman stopped and offered me a lift down the hill on the crossbar of his bicycle, which was huge fun but, oh dear, gained me a serious scolding from my mother.

Joyce and I started dancing lessons in Totteridge with Mrs Boyle, where we performed a sort of Irish jig tap dance with outfits made from green silky parachute material left over from the war. Mother found it very slippery and difficult to sew, but she succeeded in dressing us for our number. I also starred in a show as a French maid, with a pink satin tutu and a shiny pink pancake on my head, but when I was older, I attended a more professional ballet school. I walked up to Woodside Park station and took the train to East Finchley station, where I started ballet in Gordon Hall with Miss Hughes. My mother made me a royal blue tunic that just covered my regulation navy-blue school pants, with side slits to allow for freedom of movement, which, together with a bright yellow Petersham belt (named after Viscount Petersham), was the dance class uniform. I loved my ballet lessons there, just adored them. One day, Miss Hughes told my mother that I needed my first bra even though I had nothing to write home about. I was duly taken into a cubicle of a ladies' outfitters, where a lady from the brassiere-fitting department embarrassed me, measured me and gave me two tiny cotton 32A bras.

With my budding breasts suitably supported, in 1953, I took grade two Royal Academy of Dancing examination and was 'commended', in 1954 I took grade four and received 'honours', then in 1955 I took grade five and was again 'commended'. I loved to dance. I liked the feeling of movement in time to the music, the freedom of expression and the sensation of flying when I jumped.

Each year, we performed at The Scala Theatre in London to an audience packed mainly with family members. I was delighted to have my parents there, as they never supported me when I turned out for tennis, hockey or swimming matches. Mother made me a glorious white tutu for *Swan Lake*, which I adored, and a military outfit with gold braiding and fringe on the epaulettes and gold braid across the chest for a regimental jacket, when I was the ringmaster to a group of older pupils who were dressed as horses in white tutus. I loved dancing, it was my first love, and when the day came that I was allowed 'en pointe', I was in ballet heaven. I still have my 'points'; I couldn't possibly part with them. I loved moving to the lilt of the music, which was produced by a long-suffering lady who played the piano for us.

On Saturday mornings I took a tap class, which was rather fun. I loved tap-tapping in time to the music and moving round the floor while my feet tapped out the rhythm. Fred Astaire, eat your heart out! This class was followed by an acrobatic class, where I performed cartwheels, backbends and somersaults, although however hard I tried, I could never quite fully do the splits! It was a bit like today's gymnastics, but without the thick padded mats. Now, I am relegated to watching gymnastics on television and I love watching the floor exercise of both the men's and women's gymnastics in the Olympics. Like every other spectator, I am in awe of Simone Biles, the gymnast from the US, who can perform a floor routine to include a triple somersault and land with grace and precision. Magic.

Our ballet concert went on tour when requested, so we danced for the elderly, and various men's clubs and lodges. Mother wasn't happy about young girls displaying themselves in front of a male audience, but as far as I was concerned, I just loved the opportunity to dress up and dance.

Mother made me give up my beloved ballet so I could study for my O-levels. I was mortified, as I would have liked to dance as a profession, and I was sorely upset that I received no encouragement for pursuing my dreams. How could Mother be so dismissive of my wishes? I was told that if you had brains you should use them; I thought to myself that dancers needed brains to remember the complicated dance sequences. I was too choked to reply and rushed off to my room. I was prepared to put up with all the aches and pain that dancers go through when training to be able to dance on the stage. I wanted to dance. I was gutted.

Sixty-five years later, yes, you have read that correctly, sixty-five years later, I joined the 'Silver Swans' at Butterfly Studio in Navan, Ireland. This is a ballet class for the over fifty-fives taught by the lovely Caroline Kennedy. I don't look at myself in the mirror while I am dancing, dear me no, but prefer to watch Caroline perform all the steps so gracefully. The concept of 'Silver

Swans' for the elderly was championed by the beautifully bendy Angela Rippon and has grown exponentially. It is a wonderful way to keep fit, strengthen your core muscles and move in time to the music. As a bonus, we meet for lunch afterwards! This enthusiastic group have put on shows at the local Solstice Centre in Navan, though I prefer not to make an exhibition of myself at my age and shape, so have declined to dance on the stage even when tempted by fans, frills and feathers. I have also declined to take ballet examinations like some of my other classmates, as I already have three faded but much cherished certificates!

I started Silver Swans after I had finished cardiac rehabilitation at Navan Hospital following cardiac bypass surgery at the age of seventy-seven. I found that the delightful cardiac nurses, Daisy and Jenny, were very professional and gave me so much confidence, when I was frightened of moving and exerting myself. They made the twenty-four sessions lively and great fun, and I am very much indebted to them. Thank you, girls. Also, it was comforting to meet other post-heart surgery patients and see them work out with enthusiasm. We spent three minutes on each piece of apparatus, starting with the rowing machine, which I enjoyed before moving to the arduous arm machine, then the step machine, which was my favourite, to the bicycle with, oh dear, a punishing, pelvic floor-puncturing saddle and finishing with the gruelling gradient of the treadmill. We were wired up to a machine which monitored our heart rate, so the nurses could see immediately if we were pushing ourselves too violently or slacking like me! Surprisingly, these sessions were free as part of an Irish government initiative. I wanted to continue some sort of exercise when the cardiac rehab finished, so it was a dream come true to be able to join the elderly ballet troupe! I was the first member and even went on local radio with Caroline to encourage other women (or men) to join us.

During cocooning for Covid-19, the Silver Swans send cartoons and comments on their app to keep us in touch and cheerful while we are prevented from dancing. It is incredible to think that we all miss our ballet sessions as much as we do.

I used to be very fit. On Saturdays, my father would take the three of us ice skating to Queen's Ice Rink, where we gradually improved enough to join in the ice dancing sessions. My father would partner me for the simple dances and although I was not given any formal training, I thoroughly enjoyed dancing with him. Occasionally, we had a change of venue when we went to Alexandra Palace and donned roller-skates and twirled round the floor in what we thought were stylish moves. The technique was very different from ice skating, but we enjoyed the challenge and, more importantly, being together with Pop.

In the winter, when the Long Ponds in Totteridge froze over, Pop took the three of us ice skating there. We were instructed not to go near the overhanging trees where the ice was thin or anywhere where the ice was starting to crack! Oh! Dear me, no! We were too frightened to go near the edges, so we stayed in the middle and fortunately, the ice held and no-one cracked the surface and fell in.

In summer, Pop dusted off his box kite, which was kept above the beams in the garage, and we went up to Totteridge Common to fly this elderly contraption. One time, I was merrily pulling the string and walking backwards to get more lift, when I fell into a ditch and disappeared among the stinging nettles. I was wearing a sundress which exposed my shoulders, back and arms, so I was stung just about everywhere. Despite the pain, I still wanted to go to brownies that evening, but my mother prevented me from doing so, as she said that they would think that I had chickenpox. I felt that a bad day had been made much worse and thought this decision was most unfair. Still do.

I used to love going out with Pop when he went sketching. He would park the Standard 10 near some stunning scenery and unload two camping stools, two sketch pads and a couple of 2B pencils, and thus we were ready to draw our masterpieces. Pop sketched the scene fairly quickly and I was amazed how the picture took shape, though it always bothered me when he moved lamp-posts and telegraph poles! I tried to portray the same scene with all the sticky-up bits in the right place but was always displeased with my efforts, so they were crumpled up, like my raw enthusiasm, well before I reached home.

Much later, when my daughter, Claire, was tiny, I drew a cat for her, whereupon she took the pencil from me and drew a perfect feline, saying, 'Proper cat,' and it was! It was no surprise that Claire went on to study art at Goldsmiths College, University of London, and became a talented artist. She never brought her artwork home from school, as the art teacher always hung it up on the wall, and when I went to parents' evening, I could always identify her work as it was always by far the best. I, on the other hand, could appreciate art but lacked any artistic talent, inherited or otherwise, so even though I gave it my best shot, I was totally unable to join the ranks of the old masters and another possible satisfying career bit the dust. My lack of height would not have mattered, as the French artist Toulouse-Lautrec, who suffered from the syndrome pycnodysostosis, was only four feet eight inches tall and the British painter Lucy Kemp-Welch used to mount a step-ladder to paint her exquisite large canvasses of working horses.

When I was seven years old, I joined the newly formed 3rd Totteridge Brownie Pack and was placed in one of the sixes as a seconder under my friend Kay, who was the leader of the pixies. She was six months older than me, and when she ceremoniously jumped over the toadstool and went up to guides, I became the pixie leader but missed Kay more than I could say. Half a year later, I was lifted over the toadstool by two larger girls and I went up to guides, where I was placed in the chaffinch patrol.

When I was a brownie I was very keen so had an armful of proficiency badges and I was determined to excel at guides. I can remember taking a fire-lighting badge by showing a guider just how good I would be at arson, a dressmaker's badge, where I proudly showed an examiner a dress that I had made, and a wild-flower appreciation badge, where I picked and pressed some hedgerow flowers, and pasted them fairly haphazardly into a large album. I had labelled very few flowers with an English name, let alone their Latin one, so the dedicated guider took the time and trouble to consult a book on flowers and named every single offering, while I looked on trying not to yawn. My easiest badge was awarded to me because I had taken my cycling proficiency badge at school, which entitled me to the cycling badge without a further examination.

As a guide, I volunteered to read to disabled children at Winifred House in Barnet. This fine establishment was started by Mrs Hampson in 1890 as a convalescent home for invalid children. I was told that the children that I was to meet were heart patients, who looked like blue-tinted porcelain dolls from a lack of oxygen. It made me sad to see these blue-lipped patients, whom I vividly remember, who were destined for a life in a residential children's home. Fortunately, today they could be treated successfully with cardiac surgery and restored to a normal active life. I really enjoyed reading to these delightful children, who seemed to be happy just sitting quietly without moving a great deal.

When I was reading to these delightful cyanosed children, I had no insight that when I was seventy-seven I would need cardiac surgery myself. I received a cardiac bypass operation, which cured my chest pain and breathlessness. I hope that some of these children at Winifred House would benefit by the advances in surgery before it was too late.

I was delighted (I think) that my mother gave the huge doll's house, which my grandfather had built for her when she was young, to Winifred House. I wonder if they still have it? This doll's house stood about three feet tall, had a removable back and front, and was furnished with exquisite miniature Victorian furniture. Joyce and I used to enjoy playing with this when we visited our maternal grandparents in Bramhall. We would run up the many stairs to the attic, where it stood idly, waiting to be loved, alongside a trunk containing beautiful old clothes for dressing up. As you can imagine, we adored our times up there.

Joyce and I would often travel to Bramhall on our own. My parents used to buy our return train tickets at Euston station and then buy platform tickets for themselves costing one old penny each from an impressive red machine, so that they could put us on the train in the correct reserved seats. Then, Mother asked a 'kind lady' in the compartment to look after us and make sure that we got off the train at Manchester, where Grandad would be meeting us. Today, it is inconceivable that minors could travel without their parents on a long-distance journey. I wonder if the 'kind lady' was happy to be lumbered with the safety of two young girls, that she didn't know and possibly didn't want to know. I don't think I would have liked the responsibility. When we walked around Bramhall with Grandad, we were astounded when everyone stopped and spoke to us, as in the south no-one bothered to acknowledge any passers-by.

I went to guide camp at Cuffley with Kay, where six of us slept in a large bell tent with our heads near the canvas awning and our feet near the central pole. The lavatory facilities were appallingly basic and consisted of a deep hole in the ground covered by a tea-chest with a wobbly toilet seat perched on top, surrounded by a square hessian tent with no roof, so it was completely open to the elements. And it stank! The guiders gave us cocoa at bedtime and expected us to be able to go through the night without needing toilet facilities. Some hope. I dreaded having to get up at night and make my way across the field by torchlight to the smelly latrines. Isn't it awful, that all these years later, that this was my strongest memory of guide camp? On a lighter note, we did visit a shop to buy a take-home present for our parents. Everyone bought Toby jugs, but when I brought my present proudly home, my mother put it deep into a cupboard telling me that it was associated with beer intoxication. I never saw it again.

Joyce was already in the guides and when Mother argued with the guide leader over something or another concerning Joyce, we were *both* taken away from guides. I felt this was very unfair. Still do.

Looking back, I seemed to feel that certain decisions that my mother took were rather rash and exceedingly unjust. Was this because my star sign was Libra and as a Libran I was purported to be 'fair-minded, liked to balance the scales, liked harmony and disliked violence and injustice'? Even though I do not believe in the signs of the zodiac, and do not read my horoscope, I am more than happy to aspire to the admirable attributes of a Libran.

When I was in the top year at Church Hill Road School, I sat the eleven-plus examination for possible entry to a grammar school. These exams tested English, maths, and verbal and non-verbal reasoning. I used to sit quietly with my father when he was coaching private pupils at home for the eleven-plus, so I learned about the type of obscure questions that would be asked. Questions like: 'If four dogs have collars, two dogs are black and three have curly tails, how many dogs are there?' Don't bother to answer!

I decided that I wanted to apply to Queen Elizabeth's Girls' Grammar School in Barnet, not just because my friend Kay was there but because it had an excellent reputation. Alan and Joyce attended East Barnet Co-educational Grammar School and were doing exceptionally well, but I wanted to forge my own way, be independent and have my own school uniform instead of having Joyce's handed-down garments.

I passed the eleven-plus and needed to attend an interview with Miss Balaam, the headmistress. I was directed to sit in a gloomy room and read a rather boring page from a book, following which I was shown into Miss Balaam's office and quizzed about what I had read. I was also asked to do some simple arithmetic in my head. Then, I was asked which books I had read, being careful not to mention any of the *Famous Five* books by Enid Blyton, which were considered to have a limited vocabulary! I must have answered to their satisfaction as, after some time, a letter arrived, which stated that I had been successful. I was very excited and taken to a uniform outfitters in Barnet and measured for my navy-blue gymslip, white blouses with a thin pale-blue cheque, a navy blazer with a red Tudor rose badge on the pocket and navy beret sporting a similar but smaller red badge. For summer, we wore dresses with a distinctive thin blue and white check with a panama hat for Commemoration Day, when we paraded up Barnet Hill in an embarrassing crocodile to Barnet church. Unfortunately, one year, my mother decided to wash my panama hat and the rim drooped down over my eyes, so that I could hardly see out, much to the amusement of my friends as I paraded blindly up the hill.

Chapter 4

Grammar School

I started grammar school on 16th September 1952, a date etched in my memory, a date that I had waited eagerly for all summer. There were two ways of getting to Barnet from Totteridge; either I could walk along the length of Longland Drive with Kay and take a train from Totteridge station one stop to High Barnet station and walk up the steep slope to school, or I could take the 609 or 645 trolley bus from the high road. The trolley bus was an electric bus that drew power from dual overhead wires using spring-loaded trolley poles. Often, it would stop at the bottom of Barnet Hill so that an official could use a long prop to move the trolley poles onto other overhead wires. The last trolley bus ran through Barnet in 1962.

I can clearly remember when we were young, Mother took us up Barnet Hill on a tram, which was powered by an electric rail overhead and ran on tracks embedded in the middle of the road. When alighting or disembarking at a tram stop, we had to be careful not to be run over by cars, which undertook the tram on the inside. Once safely inside, the driver turned a large brass handle to gain acceleration. When I was a teenager, I used to hate cycling up Barnet Hill as there were still bumpy cobbles and sunken tram tracks in the road, which could have caused a horrendous accident.

When I was walking home from school along Longland Drive with Kay, my father would often drive past on a motorised 'pop-pop' bicycle and give me a lift home on a homemade pillion seat. I always felt guilty for leaving Kay, but I did not want to upset my dear father. At this time, Joyce gave our father the nickname 'Pop' and it stuck, so from then on, we all called him Pop and later his six beloved grandchildren all called him Grandpop.

I was placed in Miss Iliffe's classroom, 3F, along with Jenny, Betty and Jackie, who became my friends and still are after all these years, mainly because they have a wonderful sense of humour. Miss Iliffe was kind and most welcoming, an ideal teacher for the new intake, though I could not take my eyes off her pendulous bosom, which was prevented from descending to her knees by the sturdy brown leather belt she wore round her waist. Mother would have sent her along to the ignominious brassiere lady, the person who shouted loudly that I was *only* a 32A. Bitch.

I can remember vividly during one lesson, being asked how many of us, out of the class of thirty, had grandparents. I was the only child who put up her hand to acknowledge that I had four living grandparents, a fact which really surprised me. I had been to the golden wedding of both my maternal and paternal grandparents and at the time considered that this was normal, but now I realise that I was fortunate to have come from a long-lived family.

My father's father, James Blundell, was a carpenter coming from a long line of shop-front fitters and coffin makers. He built his timber larch-lapped house – Woodvale, Otford Lane, Halstead, Kent – to accommodate his expanding family. Importantly, he also built a gigantic wooden workshop holding an array of precision carpentry tools, lathes, countless planks and off-cuts of wood, nails, screws, washers and widgets. The house had an outside toilet which was home to many generations of hairy black spiders, the size of dinner plates. Toilet paper consisted of torn-up newspaper threaded onto a string, which was not the slightest bit absorbent, but then in the house the thin 'Medicated with Izal Germicide' toilet paper was not porous either. It was years before lavatory paper became sorbefacient and 'cushioned'. The outside loo was cold, dark and damp. There was not much to recommend it.

We enjoyed having tea on the lawn and playing with a few generations of kittens. One day, Alan was playing with one of the kittens on the landing when it jumped for a paper ball and went through the open spindles of the bannisters and landed on the floor below. Alan was mortified, but the kitten, although a shade surprised, had landed on his feet and lived to survive another eight lives, whilst we breathed a sigh of relief.

When I visited my grandparents, I also went up the hill on their estate to visit my Great Auntie Alice, who lived in a tiny one-roomed wooden house which my grandad (her brother) had built for her. Apparently, Auntie Alice's husband, John Chapman, an airman, had been sadly killed in the First World War. Auntie Alice had long white hair, a kindly face and the pale-blue Blundell eyes. The main reason for these regular visits was that she kept chocolate in a tin for visiting children. I have tried to emulate this but somehow the chocolate always goes missing.

Grandad Blundell always wore an old grey three-piece woollen suit displaying crutch-stained trousers (dry cleaning was expensive); he had curly white hair, the palest of blue eyes and sported a bristly moustache which tickled. He was always pleased to see his grandchildren and we were just as delighted to see him. He was married to Lily Darlington, a tiny lady with blue eyes and white hair, who permanently wore a floral housecoat and Harry Potter glasses and was always to be found in the kitchen. Somehow, she gave birth to six children; the eldest, my father, was born in 1901, followed a year later by Uncle Ber, then came Auntie Edith, Auntie Bertha, Auntie Doris and last of all Uncle Harold.

My father and Uncle Ber were particularly close and shared a motorcycle, on which they regularly toured round Britain. My father always took his sketch pad and water-colour paints with him and stopped to capture many views of the changing countryside. They visited most parts of the country, fell in love with the west coast of Scotland and thought it totally unnecessary to ever go abroad.

Uncle Ber married Auntie May, 'a village girl', we were told, and set up a garage locally selling petrol and undertaking repairs. He was one of those ultra-kind people who would help anyone in trouble and often found the bills unpaid. Sometimes he was paid in unwanted goods rather than money, which upset Auntie May considerably. They eventually 'sold' the business for a song and moved to a lovely thatched period cottage in the beautiful village of Drewsteignton in Devon. They were very sociable and I very much enjoyed their lively company.

Auntie Edith was the third child, like myself, and she was fortunate enough to be educated and emigrated to Kenya, where she became a headmistress of a local girls' school in Nairobi for Indian students. She never married. She suffered from severe osteoarthritis, for which she was prescribed an array of medication, and sadly, she died from a severe stomach bleed. She left an inheritance for Alan and Joyce and Auntie Bertha's three children, but I was disinherited because I was divorced.

The next child, Auntie Bertha, was a redhead, who married Uncle Eric, a librarian, who suffered from blepharospasm (eyelid twitching) all his life, always wore socks with sandals whatever the weather and gave birth to three red-headed children. Their first-born, Cynthia, suffered from brain damage at birth and was sadly a slow learner; their second child, Pearl, stayed at home to be with Cynthia, never married, and I was called by my aunt to be with Pearl, when she sadly died from ovarian cancer. Their third child, Doreen, married and moved to Suffolk and had three children.

As the youngest daughter, Auntie Doris was not educated but kept at home to help Granny run the house. She was a seamstress and made a meagre living dressmaking and mending.

Uncle Harold, the youngest son, was also uneducated and kept at home to help with Grandad's smallholding, where they grew and picked vegetables and fruit which had to reach London early in the morning in time to get to Covent Garden Market. I can remember seeing Grandad climb up perilously long homemade wooden ladders to pick apples and plums. We helped him pick strawberries and raspberries and placed them in homemade chip punnets which had to be weighed before they were sold. Uncle Harold used to enjoy riding the tractor and tilling the fields mostly out of sight. He married Auntie Mabel and they lived in a cottage he had restored in the grounds. I was astounded when I was shown their bedroom in the wooden eaves, as *every* inch of the ceiling and walls was covered with large posters of nude women. I wonder what Mabel must have thought, as they definitely weren't of her.

When my grandparents died, Uncle Harold was left the house as he had promised to continue to run the smallholding. Immediately, he cruelly evicted his sister Doris, who moved into a worker's cottage nearby. He then sold the smallholding and moved to the Isle of Wight and lived off the proceeds, until they ran out, when he begged each of his siblings for more. He certainly was the black sheep of the family; I wonder if he took his page-three posters with him when he moved. My grandfather left each of his six children a mahogany dining chair and a setting of silver cutlery. My father bought a chair and cutlery setting from each of his siblings and thoughtfully reunited these antique sets.

My mother's parents lived at 'Sheringham', Acre Lane, Bramhall, in Cheshire. My maternal grandfather's father wrote in his diary on the day my grandfather was born, 'Baby number 8 born. A boy.' Grandad or Walter Geoffrey Makin married Daisy Gregson, a little lady who had white hair, which was set once a week at the hairdressers and covered in a fine white hair net, in the days before hair lacquer came on the market. She gave birth to my mother in 1905 and then five years later, this tiny woman produced non-identical twin boys, my Uncle Guy and Uncle Hugh. Guy and Hugh not only shared a motorcycle; they also shared a girlfriend named Freda Murphy, who lived just around the corner in Moss Lane, and each took her out for a spin on alternate days. One day, Uncle Guy returned and announced that he and my Auntie Freda were engaged. They married and gave birth to my cousins Felicity (Flicky) and Claire. Flicky married an orthodox Jew named Raphael and converted to Judaism before giving birth to Yona and Adam. Unfortunately, she suffered from multiple allergies and they eventually divorced. Claire married and divorced a vet, gave birth to Julia when she was forty and married a delightful dentist named Karl. They live happily in the beautiful village of Lavenham. Julia is exceptionally musical and has an amazing singing voice.

Uncle Hugh lived at Cadnam in the New Forest and worked for Dr Barnardo's Children's Home in Hove and then their home in Southampton for years. He never married. In the sixties, I saw him as a guest of an extremely brave surgeon – maddeningly I cannot remember his name – who was presented with the 'red book' by Eamonn Andrews on *This Is Your Life*, a popular television programme. In Java in the Second World War, this surgeon bravely placed himself between Japanese soldiers brandishing bayonets and his patients, thus preventing a whole ward of prisoners-of-war from being slaughtered. Uncle Hugh was a medical orderly on this ward so had been invited to be a guest. My uncle was the only member of the family who had received any medical training, though I did not know this when I made the snap decision to be a physiotherapist.

Uncle Hugh's elder twin, Uncle Guy, was a partner in a Cotton Mill in Hyndburn, while Auntie Freda was a talented artist who taught art at Accrington Grammar School and also designed most of the curtain material for her husband. They restored Sands Cottage, a delightful fifteenth-century house in Whalley, Lancashire, close to the spectacular Ribble Railway Viaduct. Auntie Freda painted the 'Whalley' signs, which are visible when you come into both ends of the village. Uncle Guy had a classic open-top green Bentley, and as children we used to be driven around the Lancashire lanes in the back of the car waving to everyone we passed. The film *Genevieve* had just been released, so we imagined we were the carefree stars in the show. I think that Uncle Guy enjoyed these exciting trips as much as we did.

Uncle Guy and Auntie Freda had a caravan which they regularly took to Abersoch in North Wales. One year, while Joyce and I were in the caravan, the pressure cooker blew up. Auntie Freda yelled at us, 'Get out,' and we certainly did. From that frightening experience, both of us were put off from ever owning a pressure cooker for life.

As long-distance telephone calls were so expensive, Mother used to write a letter on blue Basildon Bond notepaper every Sunday afternoon to her parents in Bramhall, to catch the evening post so that it would arrive by Monday morning's post. She would have loved the ease of sending emails, texts and using

FaceTime, these wonderful methods which have revolutionised communication with family and friends. Grandad used to cut out the cartoons of *Rufus and Flook* by Trog from the *Daily Mail* (which ran from 1949 to 1984) and send them to the three of us by mail in a blue envelope once a week. We three children used to fight each other in order to be the first to see them. This was a touching reminder of how much Grandad loved us and was thinking of us.

As teenagers, Joyce and I travelled up to Whalley by train from Euston, alighting at Preston, where Uncle Guy kindly met us in the Bentley. We stayed in their caravan, which doubled as a guest room, when it was parked in their beautifully tended garden. Auntie Freda saw us unpack and was amazed to see the voluminous starch-stiffened net petticoats, which were so fashionable in London in the fifties, spring out from our suitcases. She announced that in the country we would *not* need our high heels, stockings, skirts or multi-layered petticoats, so she lent us the necessary country clothes of Barbour jackets, trousers and Wellington boots with woolly socks in which to enjoy our rural recreation. We donned our ill-fitting borrowed items and rather reluctantly were each transformed from a colourfully chic 'town mouse' to the muted tones of an oh-so-casual 'country mouse'. Many years later, Auntie Freda and Uncle Guy reminded us of our whimsical, and obviously unforgettable, arrival in the wilds of Lancashire!

I was very fond of my twin uncles; both had inherited a sense of humour from their father, my favourite grandfather, and I enjoyed their company immensely. Being with them was special.

Their parents, Granny and Grandad Makin, lived in a large Victorian semi-detached property in Bramhall with a stained-glass window in the front door and coloured patterned tiles on the floor of the long hall. They had a front room, dining room, kitchen and scullery. Upstairs there were three bedrooms with gloriously high old-fashioned brass bedsteads, and on the top floor there was a virtual children's paradise or attic, where we played with a large doll's house that Grandad had made for my mother or, best of all, with a range of antique dressing-up clothes kept in a large trunk. We also used to take turns riding a large wooden train, made by Grandad for his twin sons, which we rode along the hall using the pull-out struts on the antique bureau as signals. I remember playing draughts, double draughts and dominoes with Grandad, and learning the rudiments of chess. I adored him. He always gave us his undivided attention, had a gigantic sense of humour and was the best grandparent a girl could have. His mantra was, 'It's being so happy that keeps me going.' I would like to think that I have inherited his cheerfulness and a generous dollop of his whimsy.

Certain things trigger my memory so that I am immediately whisked back to my times with my grandparents. I cannot drink Rose's lime juice or have damson jam without being transported back to Bramhall, as we never had these products at home. Every time I see a blossoming begonia or cast my eye on a tame robin, I am filled with a raft of sentimental memories.

Grandad had a large budgerigar aviary, which you could enter through double doors. He loved his caged birds, but I was more absorbed with the tame robin, that used to willingly settle on the handle of his spade on the vegetable patch and would feed out of his hand. Grandad was not a well man. He suffered from deafness all his life and we learned quickly not to shout into the large black deaf aid, the size of a tin of corned beef, attached to his chest. He would have loved one of today's tiny deaf-aids hidden in the ear. Moreover, he suffered from bouts of angina, which caused him to retire early from his job at the brewery (Mother hated the idea that her father was associated with the brewing trade, even though her fairy godmother, Auntie

Nora, inherited her considerable wealth from Johnnie Walker whisky!). He used to stop and slip a small pill under his tongue when he was in pain. My grandparents had single rooms, which suited them, but his major problem in life was that his silky eiderdown slipped off during the night. He sewed two straps of material to the eiderdown, so that it would tuck in and stay in place. He would have been much happier with a duvet, but they were not available then. Another of his 'gripes' was connected to light bulbs as, with increasing regularity, they gave up the ghost, so he wrote a date on each new bulb to see how long it would last. He would have been amazed with the LED lights of today, which have a rated life of up to fifty thousand hours, fifty times longer than the incandescent bulbs.

When they aged, my grandparents moved from Bramhall to a ground-floor flat in Potters Bar to be nearer to us in Totteridge. Grandad, who was a keen gardener, grew the most enormous red, yellow and orange begonias in the corner plot of his front garden, which were much admired by those passing by. His ingenious plan worked, as he spent more time chatting to the neighbours than tending his immaculate garden. Mother went to visit him once, when he was ninety, and found him on the garage roof. 'Come down immediately,' she called, 'what if the doctor catches you?' Haughtily, he replied, 'I am mending the roof this week because the doctor is on holiday.'

Today, Alan, Joyce and I are all over eighty, so I guess we have all been fortunate to have the longevity gene. My father and my maternal grandfather lived to be over ninety, even though my grandad had suffered from angina all his life. Dear reader, I am sure you know by now that he was my favourite grandparent.

It was always a bonus to see my grandparents, aunts and uncles, but afterwards it was always back to school. The first time that I was given homework was at grammar school. It started in a small way, but gradually increased to be rather invasive and to ruin my free time for swimming and tennis. I would have preferred to stay at school and 'do prep' rather than start again after school. At home, I always had to clear the table and wash up before I could start my homework. I dreamed of going to boarding school, to be with friends all week and to play sport more often, without having to come home and partake in the family chores.

Alan used to spend a large proportion of his time in his room. I envied him having a room of his own. He very cleverly made a crystal set using one of Picky's whiskers and feverishly listened to *The Goon Show* through earphones. This cutting-edge show ran from 1951 to 1960 on the BBC Home Service, and its stars, Spike Milligan (whose daughter attended my mother's nursery school), Peter Sellers and Harry Secombe changed the face of British comedy. Alan also designed a telephone system with a wire stretching across the road to a friend, who lived opposite, until he realised that it would be dangerous for high-sided vehicles.

In the depth of winter, the dining room was warmed by a two-bar electric fire which was clearly inadequate. There was no central heating then, so if you sat close to the fire you burned your shins while your back froze to bits. In the bedroom that I shared with Joyce, if I wanted to do my homework there, I had to sit in a coat and my legs would become mottled in front of the one-bar electric fire. There was no heat at night and we would wake up to frost patterns and shards of ice on the *inside* of the windows. It was difficult, nay impossible, to get out of bed and face the day.

The only heating that we had apart from the ineffectual electric fires were coal fires in the dining room and front room, lit only when we had visitors, and a little coke boiler in the kitchen. Along with the lack of central heating, there was no double glazing. We had winter and summer curtains, which

Coming back from the maternity home with my mother and father

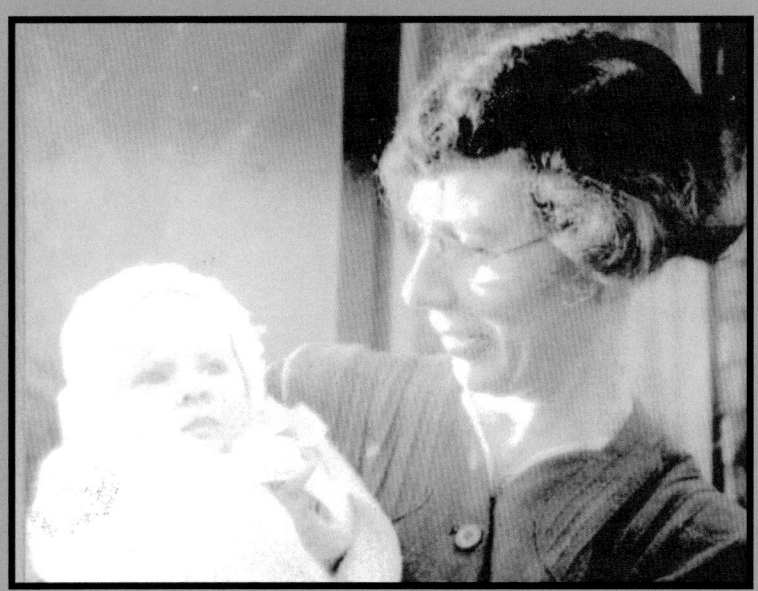

I was my mother's third child

My mother

My father

*My father, Frank Blundell, in the Home Guard
2nd from the right.*

Golden wedding of my paternal grandparents
(I am on the left in front row)

Golden wedding of my maternal grandparents.
Back row: Uncle Hugh, Uncle Guy, my Father, Alan.
Front row: Grace, Flicky, my mother, Grandad, Grannie, Auntie Freda,
Joyce holding Claire.

My paternal grandparents

My maternal grandparents

Alan, Grace and Joyce. My mother had three children in three years.

Joyce and Grace in outfits made from parachute silk preparing for an Irish jig

Alan as a cub

Alan with the soapbox

Grace with Dunlop Maxply tennis racket

Grace with leg in plaster

Grace at Barton Turf

Kay at Whitsun camp

Queen Elizabeth II speaking to Grace in chemistry lab

Tony and Grace in the Morgan outside 20 Laurel Way, Totteridge

Grace and Tony's engagement photo

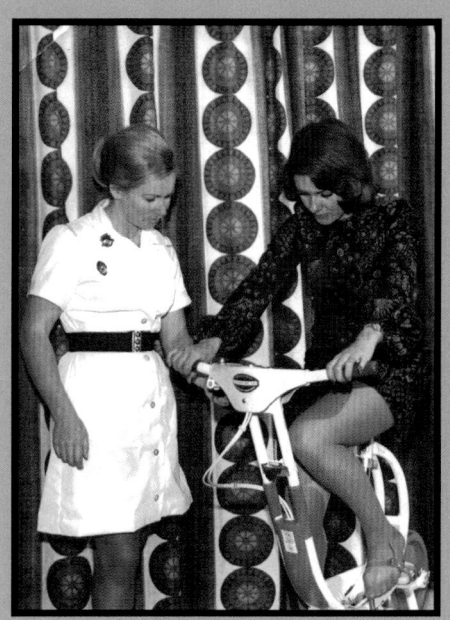

Grace as a physiotherapist

were changed with much ado twice a year, when the house was 'spring cleaned'. I could never understand how it was 'spring cleaned' in the autumn! In winter, we had thick curtains over the doors to the downstairs rooms to supposedly stop the draughts (they didn't). The coal and coke were delivered to our house by horse and cart, and later by lorry. The coalmen, who wore black leather hats with a protective leather flap down their back, were blackened from head to foot in coal dust, as they lifted super-sized, sooty sacks on their backs, before tipping them over their heads into our purpose-built coal and coke bunkers, raising a voluminous cloud of coal dust in the process. What a miserable job, which we now know caused an array of lung diseases. As children, we would be sent out to count the bags as they arrived. Thank goodness for today's central heating.

We were all allocated jobs to do and Alan drew the short straw in the poo department. It was Alan's, and thankfully only Alan's, job, to shovel up the steaming horse manure from the road, before anyone else claimed it, after the coalman's black horse or the milkman's white horse had dropped a load. Then, feeling rather self-conscious, he had to carry the precious poo to Pop's patch on the allotment, a job he remembers now without a dollop of affection.

One time, Joyce and I decided to have a couple of days off school. I had dropped a vegetable dish lid, while having school dinners, and I was worried that I would be reprimanded (I spent my life frightened that I would be told off). We put the thermometer on our hot water bottle, cleverly shook it down to just below a hundred degrees Fahrenheit and feigned a headache, sore throat and a range of other incipient maladies. The ruse worked well and we had two school-free days and were tended by mother, who was always caring and concerned when we were unwell. When we were ill, she bought us books with outlines of images, which we covered with gummed shapes to make into coloured pictures. Perhaps we were in need of mothering? And Lucozade!

We were normally fit as fleas. At primary school, I enjoyed certain crazes such as hopscotch, marbles, conkers and a lot of ball throwing, and, of course, girly skipping. At grammar school, I played clackers until my hands were bruised, and I used to do tatting, using a metal shuttle to fashion knots and loops into durable lace under the desk while in class. While many girls abhorred sewing classes, I loved them and was delighted when I received a 'distinguished work' for embroidering a border of pink girls wearing navy hats holding hands on a white tea towel.

In the second year of grammar school, we had cookery classes with Miss Dixon and made baked apples in short-crust pastry. When I proudly brought my masterpiece home, Alan, teasingly, placed it on the rockery, which is where it stayed, outside in all weathers. It is no wonder that I am ashamed of my cooking! One time, we made rock cakes. Betty was prepared for this and brought in a small packet of cement, so when all of our rock cakes took on a golden sheen, Betty's looked decidedly grey! Miss Dixon exclaimed, 'I don't know what happened to that batch,' and we all stifled giggles as only schoolgirls can.

At school, I was more interested in sport than any other subject. We played tennis and rounders in the summer, and netball and hockey in the winter. I loved tennis but was never the best at it, which upset me greatly. I gave up God when he did not answer my prayers and let me win! I always found rounders rather tricky as the baton was rather too thin for my liking, and it embarrassed me when I completely missed hitting the ball and had to make a dash for first base before being run out. I loved hockey and later gained my 'colours' (a distinctive coloured belt) when I was selected to play for the first hockey team. In those days we had a stick with a large right-angled head, not like today's small-headed Indian clubs. After a few years, our pitch became too waterlogged for hockey, so we changed to lacrosse, where we learned to carefully cradle the ball before viciously slamming it into the net. That was great fun.

At East Barnet Grammar School, Alan and Joyce did athletics, which sadly were not offered at our school. Joyce holds the record for the women's 220 yards sprint, a fine achievement, and as the event was measured in metres not yards from then on, the record still stands to this day.

On wet days, we went into the gym and did floor exercises, which I particularly hated on the days when I had my period, as the buckle on my elastic sanitary towel belt used to dig into my back, as I rolled this way and that on the hard gym floor. In those days, the sanitary towel was as 'thick as a brick' and twice as uncomfortable. It had loops either end to hook up to the elastic belt. Nowadays, sanitary pads are very much thinner, more absorbent and stick to the gusset of the pants. Some even have wings. I knew nothing about tampons until my friends told me about this preferable method of controlling the monthly flow.

While I am on the subject of sanitary pads, I will relate a story that my friend Mary told me. Her husband, Peter, had a serious eye infection and desperately needed an eye pad. As there was no suitable bandage to hand, she cleverly and rather ingeniously put a sanitary pad over his eye and drove him swiftly to Moorfields Eye Hospital. During the journey, he moaned repetitively, 'What will the doctors think of his bandage?' and, 'What will the nurses think?', when Mary flipped and shouted, 'Stop moaning or I will put the loops over your ears.'

I was far too embarrassed to tell the games mistress about my period problem, so I put up with the not insignificant discomfort, without so much of a murmur. I was happiest balancing on the upturned forms, shinning up the wall bars, and I particularly loved using a springboard to vault the horse.

Too Small for Physiotherapy

I gained my first orgasm when I climbed the ropes, usually before I made it to the top. I was just twelve years of age. I fell in love with the ropes: they never failed me! At this age I had never heard of the word 'orgasm'. All I knew was that my reward for climbing the ropes arrived with a 'burst of pleasure' previously unfelt. Sadly, we rarely had gym, so I abandoned my first love and sought other outlets. I developed a monkey-like aptitude for climbing the poles supporting the swings in the park. No scaffolding was safe from my new-found passion. I think I was on my way to 'nymphomania', but I had not heard of that word either. The rest of my life paled in comparison to my new-found delights. I knew nothing about vibrators then, which probably was a good thing, as my pocket money would not have stretched to all the batteries! It wasn't until 1970 that Ann Summers started her chain of high street shops, aimed essentially for women, with a mission statement that stated, 'We stand for sexual liberation, experimentation and mind-blowing satisfaction'. I had no idea at the time that years later, I would be a physiotherapist and lecture internationally on the importance of the pelvic floor muscles for gaining orgasms and multiple orgasms, and the use of a vibrator, with or without a partner, for women with anorgasmia.

In our second year at grammar school we were given a sex lesson by a female GP, who was a former pupil. This lesson was eagerly anticipated and we were agog to hear all about this mystery called *sex*. We were told about the female anatomy and why we had ovaries, a uterus and a vagina, and why we had periods. We were also told about the male anatomy and how when men were excited, there was an increase of blood to their penis, which made it swell to produce an erection. She said, 'The erect penis is the size of three fingers.' I looked down at three of my rather large fingers and thought no way, that would never fit in my baby hole. Talking of which, I could never see how a baby could push itself out through my tiny vagina either. Impossible!

The girls at my junior school had told me that you split from your tummy button to your back passage, so that the baby could be born! The GP told us that men would expel a teaspoonful of semen, something that I later disputed when I was left in a large damp patch in the bed. I was too embarrassed to ask any questions, as were the rest of the class, so I lived with my worries for many years. I was certainly in no hurry to experiment and find out. We were not told anything about a loving relationship, about orgasms or indeed about contraception, and we received no hand-out material. The lesson was over all too soon and I imagined that we had received the statutory forty-minute sex lesson so that the school could tick that box off. I feel that we should have been given a leaflet to explain our adolescent changes and more detailed sex advice, as this outline was clearly inadequate.

The GP did not mention body dysmorphism, where adolescents worry, often unnecessarily, about their appearance. At this stage, I had not heard about eating disorders such as anorexia or bulimia. Most teenagers hated some part of their body. I had a long list of things that I disliked about the way I looked. I wasn't fond of my straight hair; Alan got the curls while Joyce and I missed out; after I left home, I bleached my hair and used heated rollers to give my locks a much-needed bounce, which did wonders for my confidence. I hated my ears, which were rather large; I said that I would have preferred them to be rather more delicate and shell-like, to which Alan replied, 'You don't have big ears, Dumbo,' so from then on, I always kept my ears hidden under my hair, so no-one has ever seen them. Dumbo, the eponymous star of a 1941 film, was ridiculed for being dumb, but he eventually triumphed by cleverly showing that he was capable of flapping his overly generous ears to become airborne. At least during Covid-19 my elephantine ears, which these days do not hear so well but serve well to keep my glasses in position, are most useful for keeping my mask on! I hated my teeth, still do, and after begging to have something done, I was at last allowed to visit the dentist for remedial orthodontic work, which should have commenced when I was much younger. He removed four teeth and I started to have a series of braces, which I wore intermittently, as I would remove them if I saw a boy coming towards me. It would have been better to have permanent braces, as my teeth drifted back over time. While I am having a moan, I wasn't too fond of my stomach, which was never wash-board flat, and I was sorely unhappy with the generous bottom that I been dealt. When I was young, we had no appreciation of the value of a good diet, the importance of watching one's weight or the hazards of having a sweet tooth. Now in lockdown from the dreaded virus, I am battling with my weight, a perennial problem, and avoiding sweets and chocolates to curb my sugar craving and chocolate addiction.

Life in Totteridge revolved around Union Church, where my parents were founder members. We were expected to attend the morning *and* evening services every Sunday in our best clothes, complete with berets and white gloves, which was a veritable pain. It seemed as if we were made to be on show.

When I was fourteen years of age, my mother insisted that I should become a member of Union Church. It was easier to go along with her wishes than to rebel, so I was formally placed on the church register. Next, we were given envelopes in which to put a regular amount of money each week for the collection. Again, reluctantly, I complied, but the church must have thought that it wasn't worth the effort of opening the envelope with my offering, considering the pitiful amount of money that I could spare, or wanted to spare, from my pocket money. I can remember feeling very uncomfortable being conned into this arrangement.

Not content with this, Mother piled pressure on me to become a Sunday school teacher, so I complied in order to avoid an argument. I chose to teach the infants, who were being led by Mrs Figgis, the delightful minister's wife. I was given a group of eight five-year-olds in my class, who were an absolute delight to be with. I read them their story then helped them to make a present for their parents, such as colouring in Christmas and Easter cards, creating various bits of artwork to take home, and one time we even made peppermint fondants (though one mischievous boy, obviously in league with the dentist, put the silver dragees inside the sweets as a surprise for his parents), and another time we resourcefully covered matchboxes with coloured felt designs. I enjoyed being with the five-year-olds. In the summer as a treat, I took them to Scratchwood country park for a picnic and played a number of games in the open. It was wonderful to be with this age group, as they were so cheerful, loving and grateful for all the attention. I loved them and at that stage, wanted all the beautiful girls in my class to be my bridesmaids.

Pop used to enjoy taking the family to Scratchwood for picnics. He would happily fill the Primus stove tank with paraffin, pour methylated spirit into the spirit cup, pump the tank and then light the burner. Nowadays, it is so much easier, as campers have Gaz stoves, which use the liquid petroleum gas of butane or propane. These stoves can be refilled or the empty cannister exchanged for a full cylinder, for just the price of a refill. Before Mother had arranged the picnic, the kettle would be boiling so that the teapot could be filled with loose tea before the days of teabags. Pop lived for his cup of tea, whereas Mother only drank coffee, while we children were given orange or lemon squash. We had a camp table and collapsible stools and ate sandwiches and homemade cakes. The food was very basic; there were no scotch eggs, sausage rolls, yoghurts, or canned fizzy drinks. Vegetarian options were light years away.

At home, Mother always cooked a roast Sunday lunch, which rotated between beef, lamb, pork or chicken. I once went into the garage just as Pop was wringing a hapless chicken's neck, prior to plucking and gutting it ready for the oven. This unpleasant scene did nothing to put me off meat and the possibility that I could become a vegetarian was never mentioned or discussed. The main course was followed by a fruit pie or crumble, depending on the fruit that was in season, and, of course, custard, although we all fought to be the first to have the skin from the top.

Sunday lunch became much more exciting once an ice-cream van toured the area. We did not own a refrigerator, so to have ice-cream at home was a veritable treat. Once we heard the chimes, we would rush out into the street and purchase a Wall's vanilla block to go with the fruit crumble. About this time, Uncle Guy in Whalley bought an early gas refrigerator, a mammoth piece of equipment, the size of a baby elephant, with a tiny area for food and an even smaller space for freezing ice cubes. Fifty years later, not before time, he decided to upgrade to a modern fridge, and when the manager of the local store heard about his antique version, he asked if he could buy it and display it in the window, as he had never seen an antique gas refrigerator before. Uncle Guy kindly gave the gas fridge to the store, while he wondered if the new fridge-freezer would also give him fifty years' sterling service!

My parents had a purpose-built larder which we called 'the pantry' that had a metal mesh window for air to pass through and faced west, so food was always kept cool. Even so, milk would 'go off' within days, and meat and fish were sniffed to see if they were suitable for consumption. We took the mould off bread, cheese, jam and marmalade before we used it. There were no 'best by' or 'use by' dates stamped onto food products then, so we used our eyes, our noses and our common sense. Having said all that, I believe that a refrigerator and a freezer are essential items in the kitchen, and while I am pontificating, I wouldn't be without my microwave. Years later, when my kitchen in my Devon cottage was modernised, I camped out for three months in my conservatory with only my microwave and fridge. It is amazing how it is possible to cope with just these basic appliances, probably in the way that students do at university.

Our staple diet of meat and two veg continued throughout our childhood, although it was occasionally interspersed with fish. For a treat Mother bought Pop tripe, which we children thought was the pits when we learned that it was the stomach of a cow. We liked lamb's liver and onions, lamb's kidney with bacon and lamb's hearts in a casserole. We particularly like Lancashire hot pot and shepherd's pie. We often had Yorkshire pudding, dumplings or pie crust to eke out the meat ration. We never knew the joys of pasta, pizza or any Italian food, even though Italian food originated in Britain following Julius Caesar's unwanted visit in 55BC! The first pizza restaurant opened in 1965 in Soho and these restaurants soon spread to the provinces. We never had rice or went to a Chinese restaurant, even though Chinese food was introduced to the British public at the International Health Exhibition in 1884. It was not until I was married that I discovered the tastes and delights of Italian and Chinese food.

At home, we had cold meat with 'bubble and squeak' on Mondays when the week's washing was done. We had a daily woman named Mrs Waller (we never knew her Christian name – we called her Wallaby, but not to her face), who arrived each morning to help Mother with the chores wearing her apron under her coat. On Mondays, laundry was pummelled with a large stick in a gas boiler, with starch added for crispness and Reckett's Blue for whiteness. In the days before disposable paper tissues, linen handkerchiefs were boiled and poked vigorously with a wooden stick in a tin pail on the gas stove, then all the washing was laboriously rinsed in the old-fashioned butler's sink, before squeezing it through a mangle turned strenuously by hand. This was the worst day of the week and as children we made ourselves scarce. Today's automatic washing machines (and dryers) have possibly eased the burden for housewives more than any other modern device, allowing them the freedom of being able to go to work and have a career. Then, the kitchen filled with steam (there was no electric vent) and my mother found it difficult to cope, particularly on rainy days when the washing could not be pegged out on lines stretched across the garden raised aloft by a couple of extra-long homemade wooden props. When it was pissing down (my words, not my parents, who never swore) the washing was draped onto a wooden rack in the kitchen and raised up to the ceiling, using a pulley system so that it could drip down onto us while we ate our tea.

Dinner was at lunchtime, tea could be a light meal or just bread and butter, jam and homemade cakes. If we had jam or a smear of fish paste, we were not allowed to change to another spread afterwards. Life was not only hard for children but illogical! On Tuesday, the ironing was done and placed on the Sheila Maid rack to air; on Wednesday and Thursday the house was cleaned by Wallaby. On Friday my mother went by bus to Buckle and Hughes, the grocers in North Finchley, where, as a young child, I would be lifted onto the high polished wooden counter while she gave in our weekly order (always to her favourite male assistant). The sugar was packed in thick blue paper, biscuits were wrapped in brown paper, broken biscuits were cheaper, butter was patted into shape and wrapped in greaseproof paper, and cheese consisted of soft 'Dairylea' triangles or 'Primula' spread. We used to have white sliced 'Wonderloaf', never wholegrain bread, as the benefits of roughage were unknown to us. Potato crisps had twists of salt in little blue wrappers inside the packet. Ready salted crisps were a thing of the future. The grocery order was delivered often before we arrived home. I can remember once when I was home alone, that a man with a disfigured face came to the back door to deliver our grocery provisions. I locked the back door and refused to let him in. I am still embarrassed about the way that I behaved as I now know that he had Bell's palsy, which causes paralysis to the muscles on one side of his face. When I was a young physiotherapist I treated patients with this complaint with electrical stimulation.

When I was fourteen, I was allowed to find a Saturday job, so I scrubbed up and presented myself at a few of the local shops situated on Whetstone High Road. The first to enlist my services was the local florist, who I guess offered to pay me the going rate for a minor. I was shown the price labels on the buckets for a dozen flowers and prepared myself to meet the customers. Within a short while, I had customers queueing in a line which reached outside the shop. Business was brisk until the owner noticed my mistake. I was busy selling a dozen chrysanthemums for the price of one head and was told not to return the next week.

I felt no shame as I obviously could pull a crowd and was capable of increasing business, so, without so much as a reference or a how do you do, I contacted the newsagent in Dollis Parade, who wanted help selling his rather naff Christmas cards. This post was much more fun as my friends would pop in and chat to me, until the manager noticed that I was taking my eye off the job in hand. He 'had words', following which I sold his tasteless cards with renewed fervour. Despite my obvious aptitude for the job, he terminated my very useful employment at Christmas, when I had no more cards to sell, so I popped into another shop in the parade and asked the chemist if he would like help on Saturdays. My luck was in, and I was employed happily as his assistant for a number of months. However, there were some customers who would sneak past me and ask to see the pharmacist himself. I felt that I was being side-lined, until the chemist told me that these guys wanted 'something for the weekend' and were too embarrassed to ask a schoolgirl. My sex education increased further when he told me about the value of Durex condoms. Fortunately, things are less embarrassing today, when guys can pick these products off the counter in pharmacies and supermarkets or order them direct from the web.

When I left school, my mother asked Mr Lewis, one of the churchgoers, if he would kindly give me a job in his office for six weeks in the summer. He was the chairman of a stockbrokers' company and he not only agreed to employ me but kindly offered to give me a lift from Totteridge to the City each day. I was put in the 'transfer department' and was shown what to do by a man who would rather stand at a bench all day than crease his trousers. I didn't know such men existed. Real men don't care about creases! I guess he would rather suffer from varicose veins than ruffle his kecks. I was given a high stool, creased my skirt underneath me and commenced my duties. I had to look at the name on the transfer form and, accordingly, cross out whichever gender pronoun was incorrect from 'his/her/their' and 'he/she/they'. I went to bed at night dreaming of crossing out the wrong pronouns; surely, they could use gender neutral pronouns, for goodness' sake. All my transfer forms were fervently checked by the guy with the immaculate trousers, which left me with a feeling of raw inadequacy. Why was I there? What difference did I make? It was intolerably tedious, seriously humourless and devoid of any job satisfaction. The time dragged on and on, and I found myself clock-watching, an activity I associated with sitting through boring sermons in church. When the clock struck one, I went into the City armed with my trusty book of luncheon vouchers, found a café which accepted them and sat on my own to have my lunch, so pleased to have a break from this thoroughly mind-numbing job. Life became much more exciting once I visited the Stock Exchange in my lunch hour and watched the bustle of activity from the gallery. The traders seemed to know exactly what they were doing, even if it seemed like another world to me; there was a good deal of arm-raising and gesticulating, which no doubt led to a million-pound transaction or two. The first stock exchange was created in Amsterdam in 1605 which started a new way of trading. Nowadays, buying and selling stocks and securities is all computer-generated, so the feverish arm-waving has been replaced by a quick-fingered approach. I stuck this 'plum' job out for the full six weeks without any promotion, but it made me realise that I couldn't work in an office for the rest of my working life. No way.

When I was fifteen, I was allowed to join the church youth club, which was held in the church hut, a rickety wooden building. It was a very popular club and teenagers were allowed to come from a wide area, provided they attended the evening church service. Thus, on Sundays, youth club members used to sit in the back row of the church, exchange notes and whisper together. At the club, we played table tennis, danced to an elderly record player blaring out the latest pop music, listened to various topical speakers and enjoyed some convoluted quizzes. I could never understand why my schoolfriends had crushes on older girls at school, as I loved being in mixed company. I was into boys. Most of all, I enjoyed playing games such as 'spinning the bottle'. Unfortunately, one girl told her mum that we had kissing games at the end of the club night, so when it got back to my mother, she insisted that I was to be home at 10.30pm before these games commenced, which was a real blow.

At this time, I used to go to the pub with my youth club friends, even though by law I could not have alcohol until I was sixteen years of age. If I went to a dance at Kemp Hall, we would slide out to 'The Orange Tree' during the interval. The lads always said that they couldn't possibly order a non-alcoholic drink in a pub, so I used to have a sweet martini or a gin and tonic when I would have far preferred an orange juice. Pubs did not serve food then; they were designed just for serious drinkers and, seriously, the guys in our crowd could drink. I could never tell my mother that I had been inside a public house, so I started to lie, not because I wanted to but because pubs were where my friends were allowed to hang out and I felt that my mother, as ever, was being unreasonably strict. I told her that I had been to Hampstead for coffee (even though I did not like coffee). In the 1950s, Italian cafes launched the coffee bar scene, where youngsters would congregate and listen to skiffle (Lonnie Donegan) and rock and roll (Elvis) on a jukebox, a coin-operated machine which played a selection of records. The jukebox was designed in the United States in 1940 and apparently the word juke was derived from the African-American Gullah word meaning disorderly or rowdy. On the few occasions that we reached Hampstead it was great fun, though we spent most of the time in 'The Bell' at Arkley. One time, I was given a lift back from the pub by a youth club member in his white Bedford van, when instead of taking me home, he started to drive me to Hampstead. I told him that I had to be home by ten-thirty, but he ignored my pleading and drove on. I panicked. I was scared. I had visions of being abducted and blamed myself for accepting a lift. It was only when I threatened to take the key out of the ignition, which was hanging in the centre of the dashboard, that he turned around and took me home. I *never* accepted a lift from him again.

One of the boys from the youth club had a red classic car with a rumble or dickie seat, so if we raced off to Hampstead, when he drove up Hampstead Hill, it was the job of those in the dickie seat to jump out and push. Having successfully got the car to the top of the hill, we would run behind the car, calling hysterically for him to stop, then breathlessly jump back in. At Woodside Park Tennis Club the modes of transport were Lambrettas and

Vespas, and we used to ride on the back of these scooters with gay abandon and the boys raced one another to the pub. One of the rather gangly tennis members was riding pillion once, when he put his feet down on the road to stretch them at the traffic lights, and when the lights turned green, his driver shot off without him! He was left standing helplessly astride in the middle of the road, while the rest of the group laughed at his woeful indignity. Then the mirth erupted again and again, so we laughed more and more until we were thoroughly spent.

At about this time, I made a list of all the boys that I knew in the area. Out of a list of one hundred boys, I found that I fancied five of them. I found it fascinating to discover that I really liked five per cent of the boys that I knew. Looking back, was I discerning or was I shameless slut? It would be interesting to do some research and find out what percentage other girls would disclose. I don't believe there is only one perfect mate for each of us, but there is a certain amount of luck when choosing a life partner. When you are young, you tend to choose someone who is handsome and can give you beautiful children, while quietly ignoring any of their character imperfections. My advice to my grandchildren would be, 'Choose a lad who is kind, thoughtful and reliable, and ditch anyone who is selfish and has an unpleasant temper.' If only I had been given this advice when I was a teenager. How different my life would have been…

About fifty years after the youth club was formed, members of the youth club received an invitation to a service of dedication to Cressex Union Church, a new building which replaced the old and, I understand, crumbling church. The new church was going to be a centre for worship and social events for the community. Pam Cox, Joyce and I asked the new vicar if he would like to be presented with a brass plaque to commemorate the founders of Union Church, as we felt our parents' efforts had not been recognised. Sadly, he was not interested in the past and seemed only to be interested in his recent achievements in creating the Cressex. I thought the minister had shown a serious character flaw by denying the church its history.

A few years later, I received a letter from him informing me that, as I was not a regular worshipper at Union Church, I was to be removed from the church register. I was living in Devon, for God's sake! It seemed that the good shepherd was not looking after his flock. I felt as if I was a sheep who had gone astray.

On 10th December 2017, there was a carol service arranged at Cressex Union Church to 'celebrate' the closure of the church, though it was cancelled due to snowy weather. Perhaps a sign of the times when fewer folk found the need to worship together. My parents would have been saddened to see the church that they had been instrumental in starting and that they had supported so happily and had given them their social life, had been closed down through lack of support. The end of an era.

For teenagers in Totteridge, the year was punctuated by a few annual events. The year started with New Year's Eve, the time when no girl could possibly be at home with her parents, the night that we waited anxiously for the telephone to ring. In those days, girls never made the first move but waited eagerly for the boys to ask them out. We always knew where the parties and dances were held and were anxious to be included. Saturday nights were nights for going out and enjoying mixed company. I even accepted an invitation to a dance with a lad who had horrendous acne, poor chap, rather than stay at home on a Saturday night.

Shrove Tuesday was 'Pancake Day' and a veritable family ritual; the day when Mother took over the frying pan; the day when we enjoyed pancakes drizzled in lemon juice amply covered with castor sugar or, as an alternative, running with golden syrup; the day when we queued up for seconds; a day when the family was united.

Easter was a family time too, when we all drew faces on our breakfast eggs and fiercely competed with each other to be the most creative or at least the most humorous. We had an egg pan, which was only used for boiling eggs; it was coated with white sediment both from the eggs and the hard water. Nowadays, dishwashers clean the pans so well that having a dedicated egg pan is just a memory of the past. Later in the day, we enjoyed a surfeit of chocolate, which we had been given, until we felt bloated, when the sugar content changed to glycogen and caused the body to store an increase of water. Sadly, eating chocolate is addictive and cruelly makes you want to eat a greater number of sweet things.

Whitsun meant Whitsun camp at Dane End with the youth club, the time when my freckles came out and I suffered from sunburn. We never knew the importance of sunblock or covering up; the Australian 'Slip, Slop, Slap!' health campaign didn't commence until 1981. As I had such a fair skin, I used to suffer from extensive sunburn as a child, and now I am older, I am paying the price, as I have had to have two basal cell carcinomas and one squamous cell carcinoma removed. Dear reader, now we know the danger of sunburn, be sensible on the sunny days and cover up with clothes or slop on sun cream factor 50.

On summer Sundays, Kay and I used to enjoy watching the lads play cricket on Totteridge Green, as an interlude from tennis. Some days, I was invited to play tennis with my friend, Peggy, on her court at her home in Totteridge Lane. Her mother was so welcoming, so it was a joy to be there. I would have loved to have moved in! Peggy was a much better tennis player than I was, but I was fond of her and I hoped that playing against a better opponent would help to improve my game. Later, when Peggy married and was expecting her first child, I made a beautiful little silky white dress for her baby. Needless to say, she went on to have three boys! In those days, there were no scans for unborn babies like there are today, when expectant mothers can not only see if there are any ghastly abnormalities but can, if they wish, be told the sex of their new arrival so that they know what colour to paint the nursery and whether to make dresses or rompers.

On 4th September, we visited Barnet Fair, which was originally a horse fair but later, an annual pleasure fair situated near Mays Lane in Barnet. The fair began in 1588, when Queen Elizabeth I granted a charter to the Lord Mayor of Barnet for a cattle market to be held on this site. This was where we met our friends, indulged in candyfloss and spent our meagre pocket money on the dodgems, the tunnel of love and a variety of side shows. It was fun meeting up with our friends, not always by chance.

On 31st October, the custom of 'Trick-or-Treat' for Halloween was established in American popular culture in 1951, when 'trick-or-treating' was depicted in the *Peanuts* comic strip. Gradually this custom travelled over the sea to the UK and many children have since enjoyed an evening's fun. However, it hadn't reached Totteridge when we were young, so we missed out, although I have a feeling that my parents would not have approved of this pagan ritual and we would have been the only kids in the area who had to stay at home!

On November 5th, there was a large bonfire on Totteridge Green, where everybody from the area and many from beyond used to congregate and bring their own fireworks. It was always freezing at that time of year, but the excitement of bumping into our friends kept us warm. I was lucky to know so many boys in the area, especially since I attended an all-girls school.

When I was in the upper-fourth form at school, there was a large amount of construction work creating a good deal of noise and disruption next to our classroom. We pressed our noses to the window and unashamedly gazed down at the workforce and saw bronzed bare chests with rippled muscles displaying what is now known as a six-pack and, as if that wasn't enough for a giggle of schoolgirls, we saw a plethora of cheeky builders' bottoms. The men were amused to find a line of schoolgirls not just admiring their work but flirtatiously ogling at their bodies. Amelia, of course, went one further when she first smiled then chatted to one of these guys through the window at both breaktime and lunchtime, in fact at any opportunity. After a few days of through-the-window conversation, he asked her, 'Would you like to come to the pictures with me?' Amelia was elated and nodded her assent, so a date was arranged. Thus, my fifteen-year-old friend went to the cinema with an adult builder. The next day at the first break, we surrounded her eagerly to hear all about the date; when he touched her, where he put his hands, if he kissed her and whether they were going to meet again. Amelia was a great raconteur with a penchant for drama and she gave us a blow-by-blow account of their forbidden tryst. We learned more from our friend's experience than we did from our mothers or even from the regulatory sex lesson. I will never forget the excitement that came vicariously, when an intimate relationship was gradually revealed in ever-increasing detail, even though it stopped short of sexual intercourse.

Not everything at school was so exciting. I dropped history, as it was such a dreary subject in the way it was taught: just kings, wars and dates. If it had been social history, I would have been more entranced, as I was fascinated in the way people lived (still am), what they wore and how they conducted their lives. As it was, I, a pacifist, who was opposed to violence in any form, was not interested in remembering a list of dates of battles. I wish now that I had been taught history more thoroughly in a similar way to how I was taught Stone Age, Roman and Greek history in my junior school. There, we could imagine the way people lived, what they wore, how they found their food and what skills they possessed. I guess this nosiness is the reason why I enjoy reading non-fiction, the racier the better. I particularly like reading medical memoirs, as it is fascinating to read about the lives of other professionals and to see what makes them tick.

At school, I found that I had no particular aptitude for French or Latin but much preferred science and maths (until we were taught calculus). I noticed that the children who had been to France naturally became so much better at the language. I wished that I had been to stay with my French penfriend, but for some reason it did not happen, possibly because I avoided composing regular letters in French to her.

I really enjoyed chemistry, physics and zoology, and for some ill-thought-through reason we did not take the subjects at O-level that we were going on to take at A-level. Was this a cunning ploy by the headmistress to keep us at school? Therefore, I only took English, French, Latin, maths and geography at O-level. Geography was the only lesson that I shared with Jenny, as she was in the top set for French and Latin, whilst I was in the top set for maths. We were given learning cards in geography by Miss Easam and had to test each other on various data, such as the difference between Norway and Sweden or the British and French industrial regions. We did this exercise very quickly so that we could spend the rest of the time talking about the boys from the youth club.

When the O-level results came out, I was at Barton Turf Sailing Camp with an energetic group from school. My mother, who prided herself in using the fewest words on a telegram, sent me a message, 'Only failed Latin 44'. It was stark and it hurt. No congratulations on gaining four healthy subjects (my best marks, believe it or not, were for geography) or commiseration for missing Latin by one mark (forty-five per cent was the pass mark). It hurt. I knew where I had gone wrong; I had learned the translations by heart and had written down the wrong one!

I was mortified, as it was the first time that I had ever failed an exam, so in December that year, I retook Latin and was relieved when I passed.

Sailing camp was brilliant. We learned the art of sailing in the lunch hour at school, with Miss Broad using little model boats in a basin of water and blowing hard to let the sails catch the wind. We learned sailing terms such as: port, starboard, bow, stern, tiller, keel, tack, jibe, mainsail and jib. We learned some sailing vernacular like: 'Ready about', 'Lee-oh', 'Luffing up' and, of course, one that I found particularly important was 'Help'.

On the Broads, the boats were large enough for a crew of six. Our crew donned life-jackets and took out Atalanta; we each took turns at the tiller and cleverly tacked and jibed our way round the broads. Everything went swimmingly, until it was my turn to take the helm. I tacked happily, and if I may say, rather expertly, until I spotted the boat from Queen Elizabeth's Boys' Grammar School, so I shouted and waved gaily to them with both hands, leaving the tiller to its own devices. They waved back, just in time to see the reeds parting and our boat completely disappear from view. I had really stuffed up! Fortunately, the boys were able to tow us out, otherwise we may have still been there calling desperately for help. It was suggested, I have no idea why, that another crew member should take the helm from then on.

We stayed in huge tents on the Barton Turf Hertfordshire School site, in a field which was accessed through a gap in an overgrown hedge. Fifty years later, I was in the vicinity and walked through the gap and there were the large scruffy tents, just the same; it was as if time had stood still. It was creepy. Pure nostalgia.

It reminded me of the night that four of us decided to have a midnight feast on the water. We popped our provisions into a rowing boat, launched it into the water and rowed out by the light of the stars. There were only three brave souls aboard, as one friend had failed to waken. It was a dark, moonless night, almost pitch black, save for a few badly lit stars on the wane. The water was eerily smooth, without a flicker of movement apart from a little lapping, as we gently placed each oar into the inky water. When we were in the middle of the Broad, we dropped anchor and prepared to eat the forbidden fruit. That was when we heard shouting from the bank: 'Grace, Betty, Valerie; come back here immediately.' We had been rumbled, so we dropped the food and alcohol over the side of the boat and headed for the shore and our justly deserved punishment. When we were within sight of the camp, we saw that it was Vivienne, the friend who had been sound asleep, and not a member of staff, who was calling us in. We were very relieved not to have been sent home in disgrace, so meekly, we went back into our tents, slipped into our sleeping bags and zipped up, believing that we were completely innocent of any risqué night-time activities.

In 1958, Her Majesty Queen Elizabeth II decided to visit our school, as at the time, we were told, she was looking for a school for Princess Anne. (Our school was obviously not suitable, as her only daughter went to Benenden School.) Miss Balaam, the headmistress, was beside herself with pride, so we were instructed how to behave for this momentous occasion. Every part of the school was smartened up and we, the privileged, received curtseying practice.

For the royal visit, I was detailed to be in the chemistry laboratory, wearing a crisp white overall over my uniform. I had curled up my hair with pins the night before, and in the morning, it was sticking out, quite out of control, at right angles. It was not a good look. I was placed at a workstation in the middle of the second row, far away from any action. There was gleaming titration apparatus, set up on the bench in front of each pupil. We waited and waited until, suddenly, the door was flung open and the serene young Queen was brought in by a very flustered headmistress. We all curtseyed with respect. I then stood at ease with one leg on my lab stool and noticed the yummy Lord Plunket, who was in attendance. We all fell in love with him. He was in military uniform and looked like a gift from God himself.

I noticed that the young Queen looked beautiful in a maroon velvet coat, with a figure to die for, nipped in to her tiny waist. I was amazed that her eyes were as blue as the sky. I was totally in awe of Her Majesty.

Then suddenly, the Queen walked round and stood next to me and asked me what I was doing. 'I am doing a titration, where just one drop of this colourless liquid will change the clear liquid in this jar to another colour, like magic.' As I was saying this, I performed the titration and swilled the conical flask round under her nose to show her a gross yellowy, orange colour, the colour of fresh vomit. All the while I was unable to move away as I had my leg trapped on the stool. I have a black and white photograph of this occasion and no doubt Her Majesty has one too! The lovely Lord Plunket possibly borrows it from time to time.

School went back to normal after this awesome royal event and I continued to study zoology with Miss Broad, chemistry with Miss Eatock and physics with Miss Wilson at A-level. As students, we knew who was a 'good' teacher and who was not. Sadly, no-one asked us. Giving reports should be a two-way business! I always thought that the pupils have much more idea than the headmistress as to who is a gifted teacher. The head would only go on external exam results, whereas children can rank teachers on their ability to make the lessons interesting. Miss Broad had that skill, she was fascinating to listen to (and young and pretty) and I always looked forward to her lessons. However, despite my increasing interest in zoology, I dissected an earthworm upside-down in one internal exam, so when I labelled the anatomical components, the dorsal surface should have been ventral and vice versa. Dear reader, should you want to undertake this delicate dissection, lay the worm on the dissecting tray with its dorsal side facing upwards. I wouldn't want you to experience the grief that I encountered with this deceased annelid. Next, we dissected frogs and pinned them out to show their anatomy in glorious technicolour, then drew and labelled each organ. After we had mastered the amphibian, we were ready to take on the dogfish, a bottom-dwelling shark! For the A-level practical examination, we had to demonstrate the cranial nerves of the dogfish. I removed the skin carefully, put a chisel on the skull and hammered just the once and 'hey presto' the cranial nerves were all exquisitely exposed. It was as easy as that! It was my lucky day. Pure serendipity. Miss Broad was amazed and said that I should sign the 'distinguished work' book, but when these accolades were read out in assembly at the end of term, everyone shrieked with laughter when Miss Balaam read out, 'Grace Blundell, dogfish dissection.' So much for my finest hour!

I cannot remember the chemistry lessons so vividly. I know that we made oxygen, carbon dioxide and, somehow, made nitrogen. We collected the gases in bell jars, conical flasks and retorts. There were lots of experiments, where one substance reacted with another either cold or when heated on a Bunsen burner. We wore a laboratory coat but had no further protection such as masks or goggles. That said, I can report that we did not blow up anybody or anything and that the chemistry laboratory survived our amateurish experiments.

Physics was all about how energy and matter related to one another and included mechanics, acoustics, optics, heat, electricity and magnetism. I found that this subject was a good grounding for the electricity classes that I attended when I trained to be a physiotherapist, as we had to learn about the circuits of all the electrical equipment that we used.

The sixth-form classroom was situated in Tudor House, a wonderfully rickety building at the front of the school facing Barnet Hill with ancient old oak beams and uneven floors. It is a crime that this building was demolished in 1963, as it was thought to be unsafe, when it should have been lovingly restored, as a grand example of Tudor architecture visible to the public from Barnet Hill. I am amazed that this was allowed to happen.

In 1991, the large hall built in 1938, with fine wooden oak panelling, a glorious balcony and a spectacular stage, was destroyed by an arson attack and replaced with a stark modern building. This was the wooden stage where in my first year, I had performed as a diminutive field-mouse in *Toad of Toad Hall*. There were no auditions, where I had to show aptitude as a mouse, who could wiggle her nose in an alluring rodent-like way; I was purely chosen because I was the smallest in the school! I still have a little coat-hanger with 'Grace Blundell Field-mouse 3F' written on it, which I could not possibly throw away.

I was the smallest in the family, the smallest in my class at junior school and the smallest in the school when I went up to grammar school. Having a mother of short stature and a couple of grandmothers well under five feet did little to increase my chances of attaining the height requirement for a policewoman, firefighter or super-model (some hope!), let alone a respectable height. I had no idea then that my height would be a hindrance to becoming a physiotherapist.

When I was in the sixth form, Betty decided to organise a performance of *The Beggar's Opera* on this stage. I was enlisted because I could read music, so I knew exactly when to come in and play my part. I couldn't play the clarinet, flute or even the recorder, and I had never picked up a violin or cello, but, apparently, I was still needed to join the orchestra. I wore a beautiful pink Victorian dress, which my grannie had lovingly kept in a trunk for years, and added a hairpiece to make me look like a bun-penny. I entered from 'stage right upstage', staggering under the weight of a large double-bass case, and positioned myself 'stage left downstage', right in the front. Then, with much flourish, I removed a wooden football rattle from the titanic case, looked at Betty, the conductor, and steeled myself for action. It is fair to say that I came in at the correct time and gave a rattling good performance. After the concert, which drew many laughs and much applause from the rest of the school, Miss Balaam asked, 'Who was that girl in the beautiful Victorian dress?' I was always intimidated by her and felt that she did not like me, as she used to pass me in the corridor and say to me, 'Stand up straight,' when I was standing as tall as I could muster, so it was good that my alter ego had been noticed.

I would have liked to have gone on the stage. I guess I was used to performing in dancing shows and displays. I must have been a show-off or just in need of attention! I was asked to be the cat in the pantomime *Dick Whittington*, put on in Union Church Hall. According to my sister, with whom I shared a bedroom, I sleepwalked at night, crawling around catching mice! I loved my important role, where I became Dick's best friend and confidante, and I so enjoyed treading the boards that I was sorry when the last night came around.

I often dreamed at night or had nightmares. Apparently, I sat bolt upright in bed muttering to myself, so Joyce would say, 'Lie down and go to sleep.' Things were always worse during exam time, when I was known to sleepwalk too. I can remember getting dressed ready for school and opening my parents' bedroom to find out why no-one was getting up at three o'clock in the morning. I still have disturbed nights. Once, I woke up with blood running down my face holding my brass bedside lamp. I must have hit my head with the lamp so dialled 999 and told them that I had a head injury, as there was blood running from my nose. Now, poor Nick has the problem of my night-time terrors, which I believe are made worse by my medication, and although they worry him, he kindly consoles me with a hug.

Much later, when I was about eighteen, I joined The Greenroom and was cast as a cocotte in a French farce, starring opposite a chap who much preferred my sister to me and whom I just about tolerated. After watching the performance, my boyfriend's mother thought I was far too flighty to be going out with her son, so I had achieved my goal and took this throw-away comment as a good critique of my acting abilities! Any desires to be an actress would have been scotched immediately by my parents, so I put any ideas of a stage career to bed with my thwarted ballet aspirations.

I loved going up to the boys' school to use their swimming pool, even though the water was a murky green colour, which I am sure was far from healthy and the cause of many eye infections, skin rashes and pelvic floor irritations. I found that I could dive well from the side of the pool and from the lower and upper springboards, and was chosen to be in the school diving team. However, after each match, I suffered from a headache, so, rather sensibly, I decided to pull out from the team.

My friend Linda from Australia and I decided to take our life-saving exams. For the 'Bronze award' we had to dive down into the slimy green water and retrieve a brick (without goggles) as well as life-save each other. For the 'Bronze Cross' we had to retrieve a brick in deeper, denser water and swim further to life-save a partner while wearing a jumper. For our 'Silver award' we had to demonstrate our life-saving skills and in addition we had to propel ourselves forwards, just using our hands to scull, whilst floating on our backs and then perform a figure of eight. I loved doing this compulsory part and found it to be infinitely more fun than just swimming length after length, but I could never see how one could save a life with pulchritudinous directional sculling.

The life-saving method that we used at the poolside was to place the drowned victim on their front with their hands under their forehead and lift their arms rhythmically in time to their expected respiration. This was by far different from the ABCDE systematic approach of assessment taught by the Resuscitation Council (UK) these days, to cover (Airway, Breathing, Circulation, Disability, Exposure). Chest compression was not invented then and there was no cardiopulmonary resuscitation or cardiac defibrillation apparatus. Linda and I were both delighted to have passed and proudly still have our medals to this day. However, when I was swimming with my granddaughter, Maggie, I showed her how we life-saved in the olden days, but I could not perform a life-saving kick as well as I used to and we both sunk to the bottom of the pool! So, my medals, kept securely, are just a faraway memory, rather like the ballet certificates that I cherish with wistful affection.

A Quaker lady with links to Union Church was taking a group of East End children to the seaside for a week. Many of these disadvantaged children had never seen the sea and many were not able to swim. I was invited to accompany them, as I had my life-saving awards. We went by coach to a large house in Frinton-on-sea, which ran down to a sandy beach. The children went wild with excitement, from the day that they arrived, and almost immediately rushed down to the sea. I found that it was a full-time job to see where everyone was at any given time, as they were never used to being controlled. It was a heck of a responsibility for a seventeen-year-old and something that I would never repeat without more helpers than children. Eventually, I hit on the idea that they would stay close by if they buried me with sand. As I gradually disappeared from view, I counted the children to make sure that I had a full set. Possibly the worst idea now that I come to think of it, as it rendered me totally unable to help anyone who was in difficulties in the water, let alone drowning. Thankfully the week went by, albeit slowly, and we returned with *all* the children safe and sound, which was a miracle in itself. I never repeated this voluntary role.

Although I loved swimming, my father reckoned it was better to be an 'all-rounder' than excel in any one area. Pop believed he was an 'all-rounder' who could do carpentry, cobbling, grow vegetables, paint, ice-skate, roller-skate and perform handstands (not when roller-skating), but, believe it or not, he was quite unable to catch a ball, and even though he could never swim, he taught many pupils to achieve a passable breaststroke. I disagreed with this logic, as I think it would be extremely satisfying to achieve in one area and be the best in one sport. Imagine the satisfaction of gaining gold! Thus, my parents never offered me ice skating coaching, swimming training or tennis coaching, which could have improved my chances. I never asked for coaching, as I knew that my parents found it financially challenging to bring up three children on a teacher's salary.

I joined Totteridge Tennis Club and played tennis with the junior section. The adults in the senior section were extraordinarily bossy and turned us off the courts, often mid-game, if they wanted to play. How different from the club to which I belong today, in Cavan, Ireland, where all the courts are reserved for coaching children in their school holidays and adults have to play before 10am or after 4pm in the summer. In Totteridge, my mother, for some archaic religious reason, did not like me playing tennis on a Sunday, even though all my friends had no similar restrictions. I had to comply, as it was useless to reason with her, so on weekdays and Saturdays, I clipped my Dunlop Maxply tennis racket onto my second-hand drop-handle-bar bicycle and pedalled furiously to the club. Tennis rackets have changed enormously; the wood has been replaced with lightweight graphite and fibreglass; as a nod to all felines, the cat-gut strings have been replaced by nylon; and the head is much bigger now so that there is a larger 'sweet spot'. As rackets have improved, so the game has become correspondingly faster, which makes it increasingly tricky for seniors like me.

My friend Kay told me that the boys at Woodside Park Tennis Club were better there, so I filled in an entry form. On the membership form, there was a box labelled 'Religion', and when I asked why this was necessary, I was told that Jews were not allowed to join this tennis club 'in case they took over'. It was the first time that I had been aware of racism and I can remember how it appalled me. I was too young to make my voice heard, but now that I am older, I would have taken the anti-Semitic committee to task. Had they, in less than ten years, forgotten the six million Jewish people killed in the Holocaust? Hostility, prejudice and segregation should not be allowed today by law, particularly in sport.

However, the boys *were* better, so I stayed at Woodside Park club. One time, I was on court when one of the girls felt unwell, so I walked her home. She had contracted poliomyelitis and was taken to Barnet General Hospital Isolation Ward, where I visited her by talking to her, somewhat awkwardly, on tip-toes through a tiny wooden hatch. It was a very stilted conversation in that formidable setting. Fortunately, her chest muscles were unaffected, so she didn't have to be nursed in an iron lung to aid her breathing. As I had been in contact with her, I was placed in quarantine and had to stay away from school, friends, the cinema or the swimming pool for three weeks. My friend suffered from paralysed leg muscles so unfortunately needed callipers. She eventually went to university in a wheelchair to read law. Later when I was a physiotherapist, I used to treat patients who had suffered from polio as a child and had paralysed limbs. It was my job to make sure that their normal muscles were strong enough to keep them upright and ambulant without the need for a wheelchair. Now, fortunately, a drop of vaccine on a sugar lump prevents this debilitating disease.

It was at Woodside Park Tennis Club, that I met a new group of friends and where, as a sixteen-year-old, I met my boyfriend, Tony, who was seventeen. The first time that I went out with him was after playing tennis; in a flurry of excitement, we all decided to go to 'The Bell' (now called 'The Gate') at Arkley for a drink. The pub sign reads:

'This gate hangs well and hinders none
Refresh and pay and carry on'

I rode pillion on Tony's motorbike, blissfully ignoring the fact that this was not legal, as he was still a learner with L-plates. I was not wearing a crash helmet, as it was not compulsory in those days, and I was still wearing my short white tennis dress, which I had made myself.

On the way home from 'The Bell', Tony drove down Totteridge Lane and decided to turn right into Hill Crescent (without indicating), but when he was in the middle of the road about to turn, a car overtook us and hit the bike and completely sheared off my offside footrest and broke my right leg. We crashed onto the ground and I saw that my leg was bent at the shin, as if I had gained another knee joint, so I knew my leg was broken. When I saw the headlights of a car approaching, I crawled to the side of the road, fearful of being run over. A kind lady held my hand, but I squeezed it so hard that she let go and walked away. I was taken by ambulance to Barnet General Hospital, where a nurse caused further agony when she tried to undo my plimsole one eyelet at a time. 'Please cut it off,' I pleaded, but she insisted in undoing every aching lace. I was given a general anaesthetic and traction to pull my leg straight, received a full-length plaster of Paris cast and woke up on the orthopaedic ward surrounded by elderly ladies. I was the youngest by about fifty years.

Embarrassingly, my first visitor was Mr Figgis, the church minister, who was allowed into the ward between visiting times. He asked me if there was anything that I would like. 'I would love some Lucozade, please,' I answered gratefully. Whenever we were ill, mother always bought Lucozade for us, and it is only recently that I have been aware of the large sugar content in this drink. Perhaps, it produced a sugar rush and caused a feeling of well-being.

During visiting time, Tony, my parents and Alan, my brother, came in to see me. Alan peeked under the cradle at my leg and announced, 'They have put your leg on back to front.' Brothers! Tony gave me a card, which I can still remember read:

'*An accident that's tough but heck*
At least you didn't break your neck.'

I loved the young nurses on the wards; one in particular was getting married that Saturday and she regaled me with the finer details of her wedding dress and all the arrangements that she had made for her big day. I was enthralled and enjoyed chatting to her while she made my bed. She would have made a beautiful bride. I was very sad when Friday came and she left the ward. I missed her smiling face, even though I wished her well. I found the lack of continuity of the nurses very difficult to deal with, as I wanted to have nurses with whom I was familiar.

The lady in the bed next to mine had come in for elective surgery on her feet. I commiserated with her, as I considered that it must be dreadful to come in without discomfort, have to receive an anaesthetic and suffer the pain from a surgical procedure. I considered that it was far worse for her than for me. She disagreed.

At night, I was kept awake throughout the long night, as firstly, I was unable to sleep on my back, as I normally slept on my tummy (as I still do), and secondly, an elderly lady screamed loudly *all* night: 'Mummy, Mummy, Mummy.' I can remember that I wanted her removed from the ward, one way or another, so we could all get some rest. She should have been moved to a side room, as she made all the patients distressed and kept the whole ward awake.

One day, a physiotherapist entered the ward and stood by my bed. I saw that she was carrying a pair of elderly wooden crutches before I noticed her. I was helped down into standing and allowed to hop on my left foot along the ward and then helped back into the comfort of my bed. That was it. That was my introduction to physiotherapy; I knew no other aspect of the profession. I certainly did not know then that I would become a physiotherapist with a career spanning over five decades. All I could think then was that I hated those old wooden crutches, which were not a smart fashion accessory for a sports-mad schoolgirl.

When I arrived home, Tony asked to come and see me. My mother hid my crutches as she did not want me to look like a cripple! I took to knitting a selection of toe-cosies to keep my toes from freezing, including one in the school colours, navy, red and yellow.

Tony kept coming around to see me. I think he felt responsible for the accident, which had brought us together. He was working in a bank, which he hated, although it rather impressed my mother. I started to go out with him at weekends, when I had finished my homework.

One day, Tony asked me if I was a virgin and as I did not understand what he was going on about, I said, 'No.' I was only sixteen and very innocent. He rushed out of the house, mounted his motorbike, revved up furiously, and went up and down the road outside the house to make a statement. Mother said, 'What is the matter with him?', but I was totally unwilling to tell her.

For me, this should have been a wake-up call, as I had never seen anyone with such a volatile temper. If only I had known then what I know now; I would have chosen someone who was even-tempered, but I fancied this handsome lad. I was not used to a man losing his temper. My father never raised his voice. Indeed, if he was perturbed about anything, he would just say, 'Lumme', and then you knew that you had gone too far. Mother told him that he was swearing, as it was an alteration of 'Lord love me', which I thought was rather unfair. I am sure that they would both be appalled to hear some of the colourful expletives that I use today when totally exasperated!

My mother organised a lift to school for my 'peg-leg' and me with Miss Wilson, the physics teacher, who happened to pass the house each day. Many years later at a school reunion, my friends divulged that they envied me having a lift to school and were jealous of the attention that I received when I was hobbling round the corridors. I certainly didn't feel special, as it was difficult to move from one room to another. The school was not designed for the disabled, as it was on many levels with stairs everywhere and we had to change rooms for just about every lesson. My friends kindly carried my books for me, but when I was out of plaster they decided that I should carry their books for them from then on. When I was in the corridor, they piled all their books up onto mine, until the whole lot came crashing down onto the floor, which meant that fortunately this bright idea was swiftly abandoned.

Queen Elizabeth's Girls' School is no longer a grammar school; it is now a high-performing non-selective state school with academy status. I dearly hope that today it has lifts and slopes in place for the disabled pupils, staff and visitors. I contacted Violet Walker, the headteacher, who kindly responded that there was lift access only from the ground-floor library and dining room to the main hall and immediate surrounds. I was intrigued that she called herself a 'headteacher' and wondered if the term 'headmistress' was considered political.

After two months, I had an appointment with the orthopaedic surgeon at Barnet General Hospital, Mr Hochhauser, who was extremely unpleasant and officious. When I saw my X-ray on the screen, I queried that the two bone ends of the large bone (the tibia) were not completely aligned and that the bone ends of the smaller bone (the fibular) were not aligned at all. 'You know nothing,' he screamed, 'you cannot read X-rays.' I burst into tears. What a horrid, arrogant man, totally unequipped to deal with the fears of a sporty sixteen-year-old. Looking back, if I had been the mother, I would have reported this man to the hospital manager, as I would not have wanted another patient to be reduced to tears in this unfeeling, unsympathetic and totally unnecessary way. He could not bother to explain that the alignment was satisfactory and that there was callous surrounding the fracture, which would make the break stronger with new-formed bone. He should have told me that the fibular was not a weight-bearing bone but served to attach some of the muscles which moved the foot.

It has taken a few decades since then for some consultants to realise that they are not God and that they need to cultivate a bedside manner. I wonder if it is the nurses who are to blame for putting the consultants on a pedestal; I imagine this happens by those who fancy the pants off them. One of my nursing friends was running a clinic for a renowned urologist, when he was very off-hand and curt and reduced one of his female patients to tears. After the patient had left the room, the nurse went back into the clinic and said to the consultant, 'I am going to bring your patient back in, so that you can apologise to her for being so arrogant,' thus showing the consultant how he was expected to behave. She brought the patient back as promised and, give him his due, the consultant was sufficiently apologetic and contrite. Clever nurse.

After six weeks, my full-length plaster was removed by a registrar wielding a rotary saw. I was extremely frightened, as I thought that the saw would penetrate my flesh, even though he explained that the saw would stop when it hit the stockinette underneath the plaster. After the full-length plaster was removed (without incident), I was then given a below-knee plaster of Paris cast fitted with a walking rocker and, joy of joys, a pair of shiny new elbow crutches. Life became much easier once I had exercised my knee to get it bending. Gosh, it hurt (I can still remember the pain) as I willed my knee to bend by holding the back of a chair in each hand and forcing my leg to gain a few more degrees of flexion. It was like tearing concrete. Worse. Physiotherapy is particularly good for those patients who have stiff joints after being immobilised in a splint. Gentle exercises are given to increase mobility of the stiffened joints and specific exercises are given to increase the strength and co-ordination of the muscles. Once the plaster of Paris is removed, patients benefit by having hydrotherapy and they are a pleasure to treat.

I was much more mobile with my waking plaster and was able to walk around without crutches at school and able to carry my own books. I even stood bravely at the net on a tennis court and practised my shots; it was magic just to hold a tennis racket. Outside school, I could go to discos, where I wore a fashionable circular skirt, which lifted up when Tony and I jived as I spun round on my peg-leg. I remember, at two discos, we even won long-playing records, though I cannot recall which groups they were. It was 1956, so it was probably a 'rock and roll' or a 'skiffle' group.

Many friends wrote comments, drew faces or signed their names on my plaster, so as I knew that the consultant looked down on this habit and I did not wish to make my nemesis more grumpy, I painted my plaster with a few layers of white emulsion paint before my next appointment. Three months after the accident, when I arrived at the hospital, there was a message from the consultant for me: 'Get the plaster removed, then come and see me.' I could have saved myself from whitening my cast. My puny leg was released from its white casing and I noticed that I had grown a crop of horrid, curly, black hairs. Ugh! My legs did not match. That was when I started to shave my legs. Dear reader, if you can stand the pain and bear the cost (or is it bear the pain and stand the cost?), wax hair removal lasts much longer, or better still, use an electric epilator. For those girls who need dark hair removing, laser machines can do the trick permanently.

That summer, I had agreed to go on a youth hostel walking trip to the lake district with my friend Kay for ten days. She invited two other strapping girls from school to make up a four. We stared at the map and decided that we could easily walk ten miles a day from one youth hostel to another and planned our tour. We had not taken account of the highs and lows of the terrain, even though we were thoroughly conversant with contour lines. In preparation for the trip, I made a pair of orange sailcloth shorts out of one yard of material, sewed a sheet into a sleeping bag, cleaned my Wellington boots and filled a rucksack with everything that I might need. I could hardly lift it.

It was the holiday from hell. I was by far the smallest and weakest of the group and found that I was always left behind on *all* the hills and the Lake District seems to have more mountains than most. My right leg was still weak and I have never been good at hills (possibly due to an incipient heart condition), so with a pack on my back the size and weight of a sack of coal, I found it a little too challenging. The other three girls would kindly wait for me at the top of the hill, but as soon as I caught them up, they were off again, so I had no time to rest or catch my breath. I quickly learned that there were many lads touring in open sports cars, who were delighted to give a young girl in orange shorts a lift, so I took to thumbing my way round the lakes. I waved possibly a little too triumphantly as I sailed past my friends and was dropped shy of the hostel, as the youth hostel association were rather sniffy if people arrived by car. I had to be careful, as rocking up by car was against the rules of this fine organisation and I needed a bed for the night.

We had a number of chores allocated at the hostel, such as cleaning and washing up to pay towards our keep, but we received an evening meal, and at one hostel there was a disco, which gave us a great opportunity to mix with another group of intrepid backpackers who had come from north of the border. I can remember quite clearly, dancing with a guy in a kilt and admiring his furry sporran.

I was allocated to an upper bunk bed in the girls' dormitory, where I tucked myself into my sheet sleeping bag and covered myself with coarse army-type blankets of non-descript colour and cleanliness, and slept with my possessions for safe-keeping on the foot of the bed. The next morning after breakfast, all was well until I had to lift the dreaded rucksack! It would have been too heavy for the fittest soldier on an assault course. It was ridiculous; I have learned since that the things that you need on holiday are less clothes and more money. Indeed, on the last three days we did run out of money. Fortunately, I had a post office book and drew some money out, so we lived on bread and chocolate until we reached home. Not the best holiday diet nor the best holiday.

I vowed from then on, not to organise another walking holiday, *never* to carry a backpack and to make sure that I had enough money for any eventuality. Sixty years or more later, I can say that I have kept my vow stringently to the letter. After a conference in Japan, I even went around this beautiful country with my friend Shirley and a lightweight backpack, which contained only my purse, camera and a bottle of water. I have had some brilliant carefree holidays where I have not had to carry anything heavier than my handbag; after all, a holiday is meant to be relaxing, not a test for entry into the commandos.

Alan would have been good in the commandos; instead he joined the scouts and enjoyed a number of outward-bound pursuits, mostly kitted out in walking boots. With his carpentry skills, he closed in the open-fronted summer house and made it into a workshop (I originally typed 'he boarded in the summer house', but that sounded as if he slept there!), where his friends were most welcome (but not his dear sisters). He designed and made soapbox cars for the scout soapbox derby, which usually won in all categories due to his unique designs, even though they were usually only finished the day before the event, leaving no time for the driver to train. One year our family went with him to Weston-Super-Mare, to watch this exciting event take place on the promenade. We cheered for the 2nd Totteridge scouts and were delighted when they won in all the categories due to Alan's expert design.

Alan used to service and tune his motorbike in his workshop at the bottom of the garden, keeping the noise and fumes away from the house but possibly suffocating the finger-wiggler. As a typical teenager, he spent most of his time in his shed, just coming in for meals. One year, he made a unicycle (monocycle) and helped the other scouts to do the same, then they trained for many hours in order to learn to balance and ride them safely. These intrepid unicyclists were invited to perform in the Gang Show at Golders Green Hippodrome, while his family and the rest of the pack cheered proudly from the packed auditorium.

When I was seventeen, my father taught me to drive in our sturdy Standard 10 car bearing a number plate CLO 426. The number plate would be worth more than the car nowadays, but we did not know that then. We children announced that CLO stood for cod liver oil, that ghastly oily stuff, a spoonful of which was forced down our throats each morning so that we arrived at school smelling decidedly fishy. The vitamin A content was supposed to keep us fit. Pop took a spoonful of delicious syrupy malt and I cannot remember Mother taking either remedy.

I was also given a course of twenty driving lessons, paying £20 for the course by a driving instructor, who smoked a pipe which he would light up once I got out of first gear, when he felt sufficiently relaxed. Thus, I learned to drive in a filthy fug of tobacco smoke. My brother, Alan, was also learning to drive at the same time and, surprisingly, we both had our tests scheduled at Hendon on the same day. Alan passed his test in the morning, but I had to wait until the afternoon for mine. While I waited in the test centre, I read a notice, which stated, 'Candidates should not bribe their examiners or wear revealing clothing.' I was wearing a summer dress that I had made, which had rather a low neck so, even though I had no bust to flaunt and sadly no cleavage, I panicked and wore my cardigan throughout the test, getting more and more overheated.

When the test commenced, I placed my left hand on the examiner's knee instead of the gear stick. I shrieked and removed it with my other hand. What a start. Then he said, 'When I place my clipboard down on the dashboard, I want you to do an emergency stop.' I trundled along the road, when, suddenly, he slapped his clipboard down. 'Have you had enough?' I asked, then realised that this was the time to stop abruptly, so I slammed the brake on and watched as he and his clipboard disappeared into the footwell. There were no seatbelts then, poor lamb. Next, we came up to a junction on a hill behind another learner driver, who started to roll backwards. I reversed so that she did not hit us, saying to my examiner, 'Learners!' After I had reversed magically around a corner, while lining up the kerb with the matchstick in the back window and had performed a lucky three-point turn without hitting the kerb (phew), I drove back to the test centre. 'Now, don't you and your brother argue over who is going to drive the car,' he said. I had passed. I could have hugged him, but clearly this was not allowed. When I arrived home, Mother had the tissues ready for failure but was amazed that I had passed. I was over the moon, possibly unbearable.

My parents took a youth club camp every Whitsun at Dane End in Hertfordshire. As you can imagine, this was the highlight of the year, where teenagers met each other in a thoroughly natural way, enjoyed their company, and many lads and lasses coupled up. The chores necessary for a camping lifestyle were divided up between us and we could volunteer for activities such as collecting wood, lighting the fire, peeling the potatoes (rice and pasta were not popular then), cooking or washing up, all of which were great fun in mixed company. I liked to be with the boys who made me laugh. Whitsun camp was a wonderful way of meeting boys and so much better and altogether more natural than today's methods of speed dating or matchmaking on the internet.

One year at Whitsun camp, Tony showed me how to drive his motorbike in the field. I ignored the fact that I had broken my leg on the same mode of transport and listened carefully to the instructions. As I revved it up, Peter, a friend, sat on the pillion and I took off. A few yards down the field, I hit a bump and we both sprawled inelegantly to the ground. Tony rushed to his motorbike before asking me if I was alright. I was, but I never attempted to drive it or even ride pillion again.

Tony changed his motorbike for a cream Morgan F4 Open Tourer introduced in 1933, which had two wheels in the front and one at the back. The motor was under the bonnet, not in front of the radiator like earlier classic models. Tony blocked off the reverse gear, so he was able to drive this car on his motorcycle licence; however, if he needed to turn around, he used to just lift the car up and turn it around to get out of awkward situations.

We used to go to the pub, where he would drink anything up to eight pints of beer a night and then drive home, as there was no law against drinking under the influence of alcohol back then. Thank goodness for today's legislation, as we knew then that it was foolhardy to drive when drunk, but still the lads did it.

Tony and I used to meet my schoolfriend Jenny with her boyfriend, Martin, at 'King William the fourth' (Billy-the-four) pub in Barnet after school. Jenny and I would change out of our school uniforms into something more alluring, add a dash of lippy before meeting our boyfriends in the pub. The day at school was always more enjoyable if I was looking forward to going out in the evening, and Jenny and I certainly enjoyed our friendly foursome.

In the sixth form, we had ballroom dancing lessons at school, and instead of having male partners imported from the boys' school, those girls who could dance had to take over the male lead. Thus, I became a man for one day only and waltzed and quickstepped Jenny around the gym, to the gratingly scratchy sounds of the school gramophone. Our level of expertise stopped there, as there was no way that we could master the foxtrot or, heaven forfend, the tango. We all thought that it was plain daft not to have a male partner and mix with lads from our own boys' school; we could have worked together to our mutual advantage in drama, debating and dancing. Instead we were segregated and confined like cossetted convent schoolgirls.

Before Christmas, the students from each year were issued with a formal invitation to a school party, no plus one, no prom evening, just a group of giggly girls in the gym. We had to reply to this invitation formally, which taught us a brilliant lesson for our future social lives. I particularly liked another end-of-term activity in the gym, when we played 'shipwrecked', which consisted of trying to circumnavigate the gym without treading in the water. We had to climb the wall bars, balance along upturned forms, step over wooden planks, jump over stools and finally reach our destination by swinging from a rope 'Tarzan style' on to a wooden horse. This was great fun, particularly for the athletic girls, who arrived in style without getting their feet wet.

One Christmas, Miss Balaam decided to dress up as a fairy – yes, you have heard it right, a fairy – and entered the hall, to the amazement of six hundred pupils, in a prodigious puff of white gossamer net, twined with tinsel and waving a wand bearing a glittering silver star. Now, our headmistress was built rather generously, to put it kindly, so she was incredibly brave, or mad, to give this supremely spectacular and truly memorable performance. Think 'Tinkerbell', then blow her up to bursting point and let her fly down the central aisle of the hall in a massive cloud of fairy dust and you would get the picture. Everyone erupted with laughter, which lasted long until she had reached the stage. Our headmistress had a sense of humour after all.

When school broke up, I went down to Devon for a holiday with Tony, staying with my Uncle Ber and Auntie May in Drewsteignton, a beautiful village situated on the top of a hill, where the ancient cottages and a medieval church clustered around a spacious square. This was the church where once the verger was unfortunately locked in after the evening service, so he cleverly rang the bell repeatedly, until someone realised that he was there! We travelled in the three-wheeler Morgan, but unfortunately, the car had great trouble going up all the Devonian hills. I was expected to get out and push, and push I did. Eventually, Tony became rather angry and told me that I would have to travel by bus (with both suitcases to lighten the load) to Chagford, where he would pick me up. I meekly consented to help, as I would do anything to avoid a row. Later, I asked if I could drive, so that he could do the pushing, but as I had had no practice of driving in the narrow Devon lanes, when a car came around a corner head on, I drove into the hedge to avoid it. Oh dear! Tony was not pleased, nor was the Morgan. Not a good holiday, though I enjoyed being with my relatives and fell completely in love with Devon, when we visited the quaint fishing villages on the south coast and even more so when we walked down through the woods to Fingle Bridge, a seventeenth-century stone arch bridge spanning the river Teign, where we were fortunate to see salmon leaping up the river.

Back at 20 Laurel Way, we had a black Bakelite telephone with a dial and handset on top, which stood on the oak hallstand just by the front door. We were told that it was expensive to make local calls and exceedingly dear to make trunk calls, which were made by dialling O for the operator and asking her (always a her) to connect the call. Our telephone number was Hillside 7165 or to dial HIL 7165 in the days before the letters of the area code were dropped and replaced with numbers. There was no privacy in the hall, so everyone could hear even a whispered phone call, so we waited until the coast was clear before phoning our friends. However, if we wanted to listen in to another family member's call, we would sit at the top of the stairs out of sight and get the gist of the gossip by hearing one side of the conversation and joining up the dots.

If I wanted to phone home to ask for a lift from the station, I had to find a red telephone box and make sure that I had sufficient change before dialling the number, inserting three old pence and on hearing an answer pressing button A to connect the call. If no-one was there, I would press button B and get my money back. (In fact, before I made a call, I always pressed button B, in case anyone had forgotten to retrieve their money – sometimes I was lucky and collected thruppence.) Gradually, phone boxes became damaged, once everyone had a mobile phone. Many villages have hit on the brilliant idea of using them as micro-libraries, where residents exchange one book for another without any charge.

Mother and Pop used to always go away for a half-term break to relax from the stress of teaching, so once the car went down the road, Joyce would telephone our friends from the youth club and arrange a party. Our pals would come around bringing a bottle and the latest jazz records suitable for smooching. We always cleared up immaculately, leaving no trace of the previous night's festivities, but even so, Pop found out about our first party when he saw a large collection of brown beer bottles in the dustbin (in the days well before glass was recycled separately). On another occasion, we asked our friends to kindly take their bottles home, but we were rumbled when, unfortunately, our next-door neighbour looked out of her window at 4am and saw the inebriated guests departing in a selection of rather noisy vintage cars and motorbikes. When Joyce and I held our last party, Alan brought along his mates and Joyce met Peter, her future husband. The joy of having an older brother!

In 1956, Joyce left home to train to be a primary teacher at Whitelands College in Roehampton. Interestingly, this was the very college where Mother trained to be a teacher, after she had failed her first year at Manchester University. Mother had a very strict upbringing which culminated in her living with her Uncle Edgar, the headmaster, when she attended Manchester Grammar School! Apparently, she enjoyed her freedom a little too much at university and failed to study sufficiently to satisfy the lecturers, so she left and decided to train to teach infants. Joyce thoroughly enjoyed teaching and became a deputy headteacher in a junior school.

Alan lived at home while he was doing an apprenticeship at de Havillands Aircraft Company. The company was subsequently bought by Hawker Siddeley and, later still, it became British Aerospace. After many years, Alan took a Bachelor of Education degree and became a secondary school teacher, using his extensive engineering experience.

When I was studying for my A-levels, I used to do my homework on the dining room table opposite Alan, while he was studying aeronautical design. In that room, we had a clock which struck loudly on the quarter hour and regularly disturbed our train of thought. 'Have you learned anything yet?' I would ask him after each interruption and he would always say, 'No, have you?' 'No,' I answered, and so it went on, each time the clock chimed, until it struck eleven and we called it a day.

I was very envious when Joyce left home, even though it meant, during term time, that I would have the bedroom to myself. I was maturing and desperately wanted to leave home too.

When Tony was eighteen, he was called up to do National Service and opted to join the Fleet Air Arm section of the Royal Navy. He went to a number of training bases, who sent him to train to be an engineer. After a year and a half, the government disbanded National Service so he was released early. He hated the work in the bank so joined AEC (Associated Equipment Company) for an apprenticeship in servicing commercial vehicles.

Tony and I continued to go out together and after five years we became engaged on my twenty-first birthday and married on 15th December 1962 when I was twenty-two and Tony was twenty-three. I was delighted to spread my wings and get away from home. The marriage was far from a fairy tale; it started well with the births of two delightful children, Claire and Martin, but became more fraught as the years wore on and sadly did not end 'happily ever after'. Tony remarried, then tragically suffered for ten years from prostate cancer. He rang me up one day to say that he was having hormone treatment and was now impotent. At the time, I was running a trial of 'pelvic floor exercises for erectile dysfunction' and although men with prostate cancer were excluded from my trial, I was very sympathetic.

On the last day of school for the year above mine, a couple of girls decided to tie a flag onto the roof of the school hall. They straddled the high-pitched roof and inched along the length of the hall, risking life and limb, until they reached the end turret, where they triumphantly secured the flag. Oh dear. When it was noticed, an assembly was quickly organised and these two girls were expelled by Miss Balaam in front of the whole school and used as an example to the rest of us about what would happen if we broke the school rules. It was such a dangerous escapade and could easily have resulted in a fatality. Why was the door to the roof left unlocked? Why? Surely the school would have been partially culpable had there been a tragic accident. That was the only time that I knew that anyone was expelled publicly, though I guess there may have been some girls who were advised to leave because they were academically challenged. I wonder what happened to these spirited girls and if they continued to perform further death-defying shenanigans. Are they still alive?

Chapter 5

Choosing My Career

When I joined the sixth form, Miss Balaam spoke to us about our possible careers. She was very keen for us all to go to university, which made us wonder if she received a bonus for each girl that was university bound. However, she did tell us, very wisely as it turned out, that we would be the first year where everyone would get married *and* have a career. Almost all our teachers were unmarried, possibly because the war had claimed many thousands of men. Miss Balaam was forward-thinking enough to realise that our generation would all get married, have a family and have a career. Despite this, there was no career's advisor to help us to make these momentous decisions. When I went to Miss Balaam's room to ask what my options were, now I felt that I did not want to be a sports mistress, she handed me a large book on careers and said, 'Let me know what you want to do on Monday.' I am still astounded by this lack of interest in one of her pupils.

I spent the weekend puzzling over my options. I really wanted to read medicine, but I was not happy to spend five years training. My mother suggested that I should visit Mr Jenkins, a private physiotherapist who worked close by, who showed me some of the odd-looking equipment and, more importantly, told me that the physiotherapy training only took three years. So, without seeing a patient being treated or understanding the satisfaction that could come from being able to help the disabled, on Monday morning, I handed the career's book back to Miss Balaam and announced that I wanted to be a physiotherapist. How daft was that!

There was no dedicated career's mistress at Queen Elizabeth's and no tests for matching your aptitude with a range of possible employments. I was given only a weekend to decide my destiny for the rest of my working life! This was the era when job loyalty was all-important, when promotion came to those who had served their employer faithfully over a number of years, the years before 'workforce trimming', 'last man in, first man out' and 'redundancy' became ghastly buzzwords and employees regularly chased preferred job opportunities. I made possibly the most important decision in my life over one weekend.

I knew that I wanted to dance, but that door was closed to me; I liked the idea of teaching physical education, but I didn't relish the idea of having to shave my legs every day and spending time in a staffroom stuffed full of spinsters. I was not keen on going to university, as I had no idea where it would lead and I did *not* want to teach. I discounted the careers that I would not have wanted to do under any circumstances, those that involved standing all day, such as serving in a shop, waitressing or hairdressing. I discounted anything that chained me to an office, which I thought would bore the pants off me. I liked the idea of becoming a doctor, but the five-year medical training put me off, as I desperately wanted to get married and leave home. Thus, I chose to be a physiotherapist, never for the life of me thinking that I would be too small to fulfil any archaic height restrictions.

Today's students can spend time in a physiotherapy department and watch patients being treated; they can help as a physiotherapy assistant, thereby developing a basic knowledge of the profession. They can speak to physiotherapists about the range of job opportunities within the profession and the range of specialist areas. I had no insight into the mysteries of my chosen career, but that is how things were in the fifties.

I was lucky. Serendipitously, I chose a career that I thoroughly enjoyed for fifty-four years; every day was different, every patient reacted in a different way to their pain or disability, which meant that I needed to understand my patients, be able to relate to them and use an approach that specifically targeted *their* problem. Treatment needed to be totally patient-centred. Being able to improve or cure my patients was extremely satisfying and it was a privilege to be able to have the skills to help.

Then, I had to choose the hospital in which I wished to do my physiotherapy training. To hedge my bets, I applied to each of the five hospitals which trained physios in London and was successful in gaining an interview at each one. That was where any success faltered.

I prepared myself for these interviews, by thinking of the questions that I might be asked such as:

What qualifications do you have?

'I am taking physics, chemistry and zoology at A-level.'

What is your level in sports?

'I play in the first hockey team, have my silver award for life-saving, have been in the diving team and play tennis regularly.'

What activities have you done which have helped people?

'I am a Sunday school teacher, I was a girl guide, I have read to cardiac children, I have worked in a chemist's shop and have spent a week looking after deprived children.'

Why do you want to be a physiotherapist?

'I want to help people physically and improve their lives.'

Today, with the benefit of hindsight, I know that this preparation was not as helpful as being able to say:

'I have worked as a physiotherapy assistant in a hospital for the summer holidays and have really enjoyed helping the patients, particularly those who were very disabled. I am very keen to learn the necessary skills to be able to improve the lives of those who are physically challenged. I would like to show you a report from the physiotherapy superintendent concerning my aptitude for a career in physiotherapy.'

When I was a physiotherapy manager, I contacted the principal of a teaching hospital and recommended that one of my physiotherapy assistants would make an excellent physiotherapist. Even though it was difficult to obtain a training place, I was delighted when she was accepted.

I attended the interviews like a rabbit caught in the headlights. I could have done with a practice interview or two, to enable me to speak with confidence and conviction. Instead, at the age of sixteen, I tried to answer as best I could.

At St Thomas's Hospital, I was asked why I had left my mother down the corridor. Did they want to interview my mother too? Did they want to see what I would look like at fifty? Cruelly, the matron asked me my height. I replied, 'Five foot one and a half,' to which she replied, 'Precious half.' I was told that the hospital needed tall girls to be able to perform Cyriax manipulations, so it was no surprise when the letter came.

Rejection Number One

At Guy's Hospital, I was asked which of my relatives had trained at their hospital. They obviously wanted to know if my father or grandfather was an esteemed doctor who had trained at Guy's. It sounded as if the hospital practised nepotism and was more interested in my forebears than in me. I replied that none of my relatives had a connection with the hospital but that my doctor had trained at Guy's. This was not going well and went even more pear-shaped when she told me that they needed strapping physiotherapists to perform manipulations. I was now expecting trouble in the post.

Rejection Number Two

I attended an interview at King's College Hospital in Brixton, which is where my daughter now lives. I cannot remember what happened, but I was disappointed not to be accepted.

Rejection Number Three

This was followed by attending the Middlesex Hospital, where I had another unremarkable interview with the physiotherapy principal.

Rejection Number Four

I was getting thoroughly pissed off and seriously wondered if a career in physiotherapy was for me. So it was with a heavy heart that I went to The London Hospital in the East End to attend an interview with Miss Orme, the principal. When I waited in the ante-room, I had severe stomach ache, but when I was asked to enter her room, miraculously, the pain disappeared. Looking back, this must have been psychosomatic pain, which was no surprise considering my previous four rejections. She asked me various questions about my life and hobbies and why I had chosen to be a physiotherapist, which I was now well-practised in answering. Then, she asked if I had any questions. 'Am I too small for physiotherapy?' I tentatively asked. She stood up to her full height; she was considerably shorter than me, and shouted, 'I have never been too short for any aspect of physiotherapy.'

I was accepted.

I have detailed what happened next in a book titled *Rubbed Up the Wrong Way: A Physiotherapist's Story*. It was a privilege to be a physiotherapist and I sincerely thank Miss Orme for giving me the opportunity to train at The London Hospital, now called The Royal London Hospital. I hope that you will enjoy this factual 'behind the curtains' account and be amused by the congenial and at times humorous side of my profession.

The Author

Professor Grace Dorey MBE FCSP PhD has worked as a chartered physiotherapist for fifty-four years. She trained at The London Hospital, and has worked at Harrow Physical Treatment Centre, Harrow Hospital, West Herts Hospital, Joseph Brant Memorial Hospital, Canada, Kodak Ltd and BUPA Hospital Bushey, where she was the physiotherapy manager for seventeen years. She also ran a private practice in Chesham Bois and Harley Street. She set up a continence clinic at the Somerset Nuffield Hospital, Taunton and at North Devon District Hospital, Barnstaple. Following the stunning result of her PhD research titled 'Pelvic Floor Exercises for Erectile Dysfunction', Grace has lectured internationally. She is the author of three textbooks and eight self-help books. Recently, she has written her physiotherapy memoirs.

She has a daughter, a son and two granddaughters, and lives in Ireland with her partner, Nick.

She wrote this book while she was cocooned from Covid-19.

Acknowledgements

I would like to thank Pop for always being there for me.

I am indebted to my mother for helping me to choose such a fulfilling career.

My childhood was coloured brighter by having a brother and a sister to share it with. A sincere thank you to Alan and Joyce.

To my partner, Nick, thank you for everything.

Other Books by the Same Author

Rubbed Up the Wrong Way: A Physiotherapist's Story
Unsurprisingly, this is the sequel to *Too Small for Physiotherapy* and relates the trials and tribulations of a career in physiotherapy with many interesting, amusing and poignant anecdotes. It follows the pathway of a diminutive physiotherapist throughout fifty-seven years in the profession, as she recalls her lack of knowledge in her chosen career to her pathway from a basic grade physiotherapist in the NHS, to an occupational physiotherapist, to a private practitioner, to a physiotherapy manager in a private hospital, and ultimately to becoming a university professor and an international lecturer. Her proudest moment was receiving an MBE (and a laugh) from HRH Prince Charles at Buckingham Palace. In this book, she shares the congenial and at times humorous side of her profession.

Barking Mad in Barnstaple
The diary of an elderly professor of physiotherapy, who was given a fluffy golden retriever puppy by her partner for Christmas and who adamantly believed that puppy training was easy and would produce the perfect dog. William remained uncontrolled despite diligently attending all the dog training classes available in Devon and the surrounding counties.

William: Still Barking
This book continues to monitor the 'hound from hell' and recalls how the local farmer threatened to shoot him, how he exterminated rabbits, birds and mice, how the grandchildren were frightened of him and how the family were concerned that an uncontrolled dog, the size of a rogue elephant, would be too strong for his owner.

A Puppy the Size of a Pony
This is a sequel to *Barking Mad in Barnstaple* and *William: Still Barking* and completes the trilogy by Grace Dorey, which continues to monitor this rogue retriever while he grapples with his determination to escape, hones his hunting skills by chasing foxes, pheasants and deer, and displays a passionate love affair with anything muddy. Despite all his numerous imperfections, and there are many, he forms a special bond with his owner, so that she finds it a privilege to love and own a zany, hair-brained comedian called 'William'.

Don't Expect the Vet to Laugh
This lively and amusing book follows the path of two gorgeous black flat coat retrievers from puppyhood to something resembling adulthood and includes their many foibles and wayward characteristics. It includes their friendship with William, the star of three previous books, until mayhem rules and threatens to exasperate their normally cheerful owner.

Other Books by the Same Author

Clench It or Drench It!
Self-help book for women with urinary leakage.

Love Your Gusset: Making Friends with Your Pelvic Floor
Cartoon book for women with incontinence, sexual dysfunction and an outrageous sense of humour.

Make It or Fake It!
Self-help book for women with sexual dysfunction.

Prevent It!
Guide for men and women with leakage from the back passage.

Use It or Lose It!
Self-help book for men with urinary leakage and erectile dysfunction.

Living and Loving After Prostate Surgery
Self-help book for men with incontinence and erectile dysfunction after prostate surgery.

Stronger and Longer!
Guide on improving erections with pelvic floor exercises.

Pump Up Your Penis: Easy Exercises to Strengthen Your Erection
Cartoon book for men with erectile dysfunction and a wild sense of humour.

Conservative Treatment of Male Urinary Incontinence and Erectile Dysfunction
Textbook.

Pelvic Dysfunction in Men: Diagnosis and Treatment of Male Incontinence and Erectile Dysfunction
Textbook.

Pelvic Floor Exercises for Erectile Dysfunction
Textbook